WAY OF THE
TURTLE

CURTIS M. FAITH

McGraw-Hill

New York   Chicago   San Francisco   Lisbon   London   Madrid   Mexico City
Milan   New Delhi   San Juan   Seoul   Singapore   Sydney   Toronto

The **McGraw·Hill** Companies

7 8 9 0 DOC/DOC 0

ISBN-13: 978-0-07-148664-4
ISBN-10: 0-07-148664-X

McGraw-Hill books are available at special discounts to use as premiums and sales promotions, or for use in corporate training programs. For more information, please write to the Director of Special Sales, Professional Publishing, McGraw-Hill, Two Penn Plaza, New York, NY 10121-2298. Or contact your local bookstore.

This book is printed on acid-free paper.

Library of Congress Cataloging-in-Publication Data
Faith, Curtis.
 The way of the turtle / by Curtis Faith.
  p. cm.
 ISBN 0-07-148664-X (alk. paper)
 1. Futures. 2. Portfolio management. I. Title.
 HG6024.A3F16   2007
 332.64'52—dc22
                    2007000658

To
Richard Dennis, who made it all possible,
and to
Juliet Mantiply, my first muse;
may our paths cross again some day.

ACKNOWLEDGMENTS

Although I have learned from almost everyone I have interacted with over the years, there are a few people I want to thank especially for their contributions to *Way of the Turtle*.

First and foremost, I am greatly indebted to Richard Dennis, who had the balls to propose and execute the Turtle idea. I am also grateful for his confidence in me and my abilities when I was only 19 years of age. Richard is one of the modern era's truly great traders. He is also one of the most courageous. He is a thoughtful, honest, and genuine person. I am honored to have learned from him.

Second, I want to thank Rotchy Barker, who was my first trading mentor. He took me into his home and taught me for no other reason than that he believed in me. Rotchy is the genuine article: a very generous and honest man and an excellent trader. I learned much of value from Rotchy, not the least of which is that all successful people owe their success to the help of others. I hope my own life honors that spirit.

Third, I want to thank George Arndt for having the crazy notion that 17-year-old kids could program computers long before that was a well-known idea. But most of all, he gets credit for instilling in me his passion for trading and for persuading me to apply for the position with Richard Dennis.

These three men helped set me down the path that became the Turtle legend and provided the basis for this book. Many others have helped me in the writing of this book.

Dalia Al-Othman, my dulce de leche and dear friend, helped me get my prose in decent shape for submission to my editor. She was also there helping me along and encouraging me whenever I was discouraged. Thank you, Dalia.

Jeanne Glasser, my editor, was terrific fun to work with. She is largely responsible for the readability of this manuscript. The story flows and the words come together because of Jeanne. The book would not have been finished without her persistent guidance and nudging. Thank you, Jeanne.

Tim Arnold is my longtime friend and business associate; and the guy who now runs Trading Blox, LLC, the trading software company I founded a few years back. Writing this book has taken away from the time I normally would have committed to that business. Tim patiently filled in the gaps I created by being dedicated to writing this book over the last six months. Without Tim's help it would have been impossible to write it. Thank you, Tim.

There are few people in the world who do as much thinking about trading and as much sharing of their knowledge as Mark Johnson, who runs MGJ Capital Management, LLC. Mark has contributed an amazing number of postings to online discussion groups and forums over the last several years that have made me think. Many of the changes in my own thinking started with a seed planted by Mark, a seed that made me challenge what I had been doing. Mark first gave me the idea behind RAR% and much of what became R-cubed. Mark created the basis for the ATR channel breakout system when he published his PGO system a few years back. Mark also spent time reviewing this manuscript and gave me important and detailed feedback, including pointing out assumptions I had made that might not be obvious to new readers. The book is much better because of his suggestions. Thank you, Mark.

Tom Rollinger came to me several years back and asked me to teach him how to trade. I was impressed with his single-minded pursuit of the goal of being a great trader. His determination was the impetus that got me to return to trading after a 15-year hiatus. I would not be writing this book had he not come to me. Thank you, Tom.

I would also like to thank everyone who took the time to read early copies of the manuscript and give me honest feedback: Brett Steenbarger, a trader and author who runs a trading blog at http://traderfeed.blogspot.com; Mike Taylor, who runs the blog at http://taylortree.com; David Bromley, who runs the trading education company Modus Trading (http://www.modustrading.com); John Knott; Anthony Garner; and Jennifer Scofield.

Finally, I want to thank Van Tharp and Melita Hunt for recommending me to McGraw-Hill as a potential new author. And Van for taking the time out of his very busy schedule to read my book on short notice, for his candid feedback, and for writing a very nice foreword. This means a lot to me. Thank you, Van and Melita.

CONTENTS

FOREWORD

I had just finished writing the second edition of my book *Trade Your Way to Financial Freedom* when my editor asked me who I'd recommend as a new author for McGraw-Hill. The first person who popped into my mind was Curtis Faith. Curtis had been the most successful of the Turtles.

After the initial training period, Curtis was the only trader who had totally captured the biggest trend during that time period. He traded the largest account for Richard Dennis, making over $31 million for Dennis while he was a Turtle, reported Stanley Angrist in the *Wall Street Journal*. Also, Curtis, much like me, has followed a road less traveled since he ended his Turtle career, and that path suggests that he is in tune with himself instead of with Main Street or Wall Street.

Who better to write a book for McGraw-Hill than someone like that? I didn't think anything more about it until I was asked to supply a quote about a new book called *Way of the Turtle*. Lo and behold, it was Curtis's book. I read about seventy pages of the unedited galleys and immediately decided that the book needed a foreword and that I really wanted to write it. Why? In my opinion, *this is one of the five best trading books ever written,* and I will recommend that all my clients become familiar with its contents.

I almost became one of the first Turtles, and so I have always followed the success of the Turtles with particular interest. In September 1983 I began my business of coaching traders. It was a part-time endeavor since I still was working as a research psychologist. Nevertheless, by 1983 I considered myself a pretty good trading coach. I had developed a test for determining a person's trading ability that was a good predictor of success; I called it the Investment Psychology Inventory. Lots of traders had taken it, saying that they agreed with my assessment of their strengths and weaknesses.

It was at about that time that I saw a full-page ad from Richard Dennis in a major newspaper. He was going to select ten or so traders, train them in his methods, and then give each of them a million dollars of his money to trade. The offer was so good that I expected that thousands of people would apply. As a result, I thought it was a great opportunity for me to help them with the Investment Psychology Inventory. They'd be screening thousands of people, and I could help. As a result, I contacted the offices at C&D Commodities in Chicago and sent them a copy of the test. Both Dale Dellutri (C&D's business manager) and Richard Dennis took the tests, but that was as far as it got.

However, they sent me a copy of their screening test, which consisted of sixty-three true/false questions and eleven short answer questions. The questions were somewhat like the following:

T/F The majority of traders are always wrong. (The word *always* makes that one tough to answer.)

Name a risky thing you have done and why.

I was curious about the test and sent it in with my answers. To my surprise, I got an invitation to interview for a Turtle position in Chicago, where I was asked many questions, such as, "If markets are random, how can anyone make money trading?" I'm not sure how I answered that one, but it probably wasn't the way I would answer it now. I was told that ten people would be selected from the forty applicants to train under Richard Dennis and Bill Eckhardt. We then would sign a contract for five years that could be terminated at any time for lack of performance.

I was not selected to be among the final ten, and I can understand why. I was terribly conflicted over the position. I had gotten involved only because I wanted to help C&D Commodities with the testing. I lived in southern California, and the last thing I wanted to do was move to Chicago for five years. I was sure I would have to leave my wife and son in California if I did that, although that's just speculation. I loved what I was doing—developing a new business as a trading coach—and although becoming a Turtle might have been very valuable in launching that career, I didn't want to give up my coaching. Lastly, I didn't want to go to Chicago for the last two weeks of the year (Christmas and New Year's) for the training. I think that conflict showed up pretty clearly in the interview, and I was not selected.

Nevertheless, I had some regret at not being selected, especially when I learned of the success of the Turtles. As a result, I've always been fascinated to know what they learned. Over the years, I've talked extensively with several of them and learned the essence of how they traded. I teach a more general form of their position sizing algorithm in my systems class and in my book *The Definitive Guide to Expectancy and Position Sizing*. I've never thought that the systems they used are anything special. In my opinion, their success was due entirely to their psychology and their position sizing. The Turtles were held to secrecy for a period of ten years, and that kind of veil makes the mystery of what they did even more intriguing. Most people believe that they must have had some magic secret and that no one is going to reveal it, ever.

Why do I believe that *Way of the Turtles* is one of the five best trading books ever written?

First, it paints a very clear picture of what is necessary for trading success. Curtis says in very concise terms that it's not about the trading system; it's about the trader's ability to execute the trading system. Curtis earned $78,000 in the initial training period, which was almost three times as much as the others earned, yet they all had been taught to do the same thing. Why had ten people who all were taught a certain set of rules, including fixed position sizing rules, produced different results? Curtis said that some of the other Turtles thought that Richard had given him special information, but Curtis and I know that the answer is that trading psychology produced the difference in the results.

When I was trained in psychology in the late 1960s, the emphasis was on behaviorism. The psychology curriculum was designed to develop rules to answer the question: If you stimulate someone in a particular way, how will that person respond? In my opinion, that approach was rubbish, and I was delighted when researchers started to study the psychology of risk. The eventual conclusion of that research is that human beings take many shortcuts in their decision making and that makes them very inefficient decision makers. Since that time, an entire field of behavioral economics has developed out of that research.

The second truly fascinating aspect of *Way of the Turtle* is that it probably has the most lucid description of how some of the principles of behavioral finance apply to and influence trading that I've ever read. Curtis even goes into a lengthy discussion of support and resistance and why they exist because of inefficiencies in our decision making. *It is must-read material.*

The third aspect of *Way of the Turtle* that I really like is its emphasis on game theory and the way it uses game theory to explain how a trader should think. For example, the idea is to concentrate on present trading, forgetting the past and the future. Why? Because you know from your historical testing that you probably will be wrong most of the time but that your gains will be much larger than your losses. This will result in a positive expectation. Curtis tells the readers why they must understand and have confidence in the expectation of their systems. It's that confidence that will make them long-term winners.

Other excellent topics include:

- How the Turtles were trained and what they actually learned.

- The real "secrets" of the Turtles (I've already given you lots of clues).

- An excellent discussion of the problems involved with system development and why people make mistakes in system development because they don't understand the basic statistical principles involved in sampling theory.

- A superb discussion of why most systems fail to perform adequately. Even though most good systems are dropped for psychological reasons, there are many bad systems out there that look good at first glance. If you want to know why they look good and how to spot them, you must read this book.

- Finally, there is an interesting discussion of robust measures of systems. If you understand this material, you will have gone a long way toward being able to design a profitable long-term system for yourself that will work.

Put all of this together with a number of stories about Curtis's experiences as a Turtle, plus his amazing ability to synthesize his experiences as a trader and get to the essence of what is important, and you have a book that is a must-read for all traders or anyone who has considered putting his or her money into the markets.

The Turtle program began as a bet between Richard Dennis and Bill Eckhardt over whether trading can be taught. Richard was willing to stake his own money on the idea that trading can be taught. In *Way of the Turtle*, Curtis gives his opinion about the outcome of that bet (it might not be what you think), but when you read his opinion, I'd like you to think about one more thing: Forty people were interviewed from over a thousand applicants, and only a portion of those forty were selected. Combine that with what Curtis says about sampling and I think you have the real answer to the question of whether anyone can learn to trade.

Van K. Tharp, Ph.D.
Trading Coach
President, The Van Tharp Institute

PREFACE

A little more than 20 years ago, I was part of a grand experiment that has become legendary among traders and investors. Known simply as the Turtles, the experiment started as a bet between two famous traders who were also friends: Richard Dennis and William Eckhardt.

This is my story of that time and what I have learned since then. I hope that eventually one of the other Turtles will write a more comprehensive account of that period. This is not that kind of book. At age 19, I was too much of an outsider to be in a position now to discuss our collective experience. I was also too young to appreciate much of the social interaction that occurred within the group as we worked together and competed for survival as Turtles.

What follows is a portrayal of what I experienced and learned as a Turtle. *Way of the Turtle* lays bare the entire experiment, explaining exactly what we were taught and how we traded. The book details some of our biggest trades and the rules behind their timing, delivering insights into what it takes to make millions in the markets. For me, *Way of the Turtle* is a story of trading and of life, specifically, how looking at life the way a great trader does can bring you more joy, a greater range of experience, and far less regret.

The chapters that follow will examine this perspective as well as the following topics:

- **How the Turtles made money:** What it was at the core of the Turtle trading approach that allowed me to earn more than 100 percent returns for the four-plus years of the Turtle program

- **Why some Turtles made more money than others:** How the approach allowed some to be successful while others with the exact same knowledge lost money

- **How the Turtle Way applies to stocks and Forex:** How to look beyond the rules as we implemented them to find core strategies that work for any tradable market

- **How you can apply the Turtle Way to your own trades and in your own life**

INTRODUCTION

The Day I Met the Prince of the Pits

In your lifetime you can expect to experience only a handful of defining moments. I had two in one day at the age of 19: seeing the Art Deco building that is home to the Chicago Board of Trade (CBOT) for the first time and meeting Richard Dennis, the legendary commodities trader.

The CBOT is the most famous vista in Chicago. From even a mile away, you can see the building at 141 West Jackson Boulevard crowned by a lone statue of Ceres, the Roman goddess of agriculture. At forty-five stories high, framed by other skyscrapers, the building stands tall among its brethren and is a fitting home for the Exchange. Inside are the pits where traders stand shoulder to shoulder buying and selling millions of dollars' worth of grains, meats, and currencies every few seconds amid shouts and elaborate signaling. Organized pandemonium of this sort leaves the thousands of outsiders who visit the pits every year in awe. For traders, it is Mecca.

As I stepped into the elevator at 141 Jackson, my palms began to sweat. I was 19 years old and about to have an interview with Richard

Dennis, one of the world's most famous commodities speculators. Even before the Turtle experiment became widely known, Dennis had earned a place in trading lore. He was branded the Prince of the Pits; that moniker acknowledged his feat in turning a few thousand dollars into several hundred million by his mid-thirties.

I later learned how lucky I was to be on that elevator. Over 1,000 people had applied for the position for which I was interviewing, and only 40 applicants had been granted an audience with Dennis. Only 13 — less than 1 in 100 — ultimately were chosen, with another 10 selected for a follow-on program the next year.

Long before Donald Trump's *The Apprentice* and other reality television contests aired, Dennis created his own competition, prompted by a debate between him and his good friend — and an equally successful trader — William (Bill) Eckhardt about whether great traders are made or born. Dennis believed he could transform almost anyone into a winning trader; Eckhardt believed it was a matter of nature, not nurture. Dennis put his money where his mouth was, and the two made a wager.

To settle the bet, they took out large ads in the *Wall Street Journal*, *Barron's*, and the *New York Times* announcing that Dennis was accepting applications from people interested in becoming his trainees. The ad further stated that he would teach this group his trading methods and give each trainee a million-dollar trading account.

At the time, I didn't understand the significance of the ad. In placing it and proceeding with the bet, Dennis had made a bold statement. He believed that he understood the reasons for his own success so well that he could teach others to trade just as well — even if they were total strangers who never had traded before. He was so confident in that assertion that he was willing to risk millions of his own cash to prove it.

Dennis's trainees — of whom I was one — came to be known as the Turtles after their success became a trading legend. Over four and a half years the Turtles earned an average return of over 80 percent per year. But why the name *Turtles?* That name comes from the place where Dennis and Eckhardt stood when the long-running debate turned serious: a turtle farm in Singapore. Seeing the turtle farm up close, Dennis reportedly blurted out, "We're going to raise traders like they raise turtles in Singapore."

So there I was, age 19, palms sweating, on the verge of meeting the Prince of the Pits. Walking down the hallway, I shouldn't have been surprised by the utilitarian look of the offices. There was no grand entrance, no fancy lobby, no attempt to impress clients, brokers, or any other kind of bigwig. Dennis was known for not wasting money on showy display, and so the frugal surroundings made sense; even so, I expected more. Everything seemed smaller than I had envisioned.

I found the door with the nameplate "C & D Commodities" and opened it.

Dale Deluttri, Dennis's business manager, greeted me at the door and told me that Richard was finishing another interview. I already knew what Richard looked like, having seen his photo in a few articles, but I did not have a clear insight into his personality, and so I passed the time worrying about that.

In preparation for the interview I had read everything I could find on or about Richard, and so I did have a few clues about his personality but not as much as I wanted. I also had taken Richard's 40-question test (that was part of the application), and so I knew something about what he considered important in a trader.

When the door to Richard's office opened, the previous candidate exited, told me a bit about his interview, and wished me luck. He must have done well; I saw him a few weeks later at the first training class. I walked in and met Richard and his partner, William Eckhardt—Rich and Bill as we would later call them and as I still think of them. Rich was a mountain of a guy with a friendly face and a quiet manner. Bill was thin and of average height. He looked and dressed like a professor of applied mathematics at the University of Chicago.

The interview paralleled the written test that I had received from Rich's C&D Commodities as part of the application process. Rich was interested in my theory of the markets and why I thought money could be made by trading. They were both very interested in the specifics of my background. Looking back on it now, I was an aberration. Even today very few people have the specific experience I had at 19 years of age, at least as it related to the trading methods we were later taught.

In the fall of 1983 few people had personal computers; in fact, PCs had just been invented. Yet for the previous two years I had been programming the Apple II computer as a part-time job after school. I programmed the computer to analyze what were then known as *systems*: trading strategies with specific rules that defined exactly when to buy and sell stocks or commodities on the basis of their price movement. During those two years I had written 30 or 40 different programs that tested trading systems through the use of historical data to determine how much money would have been made if those systems had been used in various markets. I later realized that this was cutting-edge research in 1983.

What had begun as an interesting after-school job evolved into a passion. I was working for a company called Harvard Investment Service that was located in the kitchen of a small house in the town of Harvard, Massachusetts, about 40 miles west of Boston. Harvard is the quintessential New England small town: apple orchards, a small library, a town hall, and the town square. Harvard Investment Service consisted of just three people: George Arndt (who owned the kitchen and the company and told us what to do), my friend Tim Arnold, and me. Tim and I did the grunt work.

George had been the first one to interest me in trading. He had lent me his personal copy of *Reminiscences of a Stock Operator*, Edwin Lefèvre's fictional biography of the famous speculator Jesse Livermore. I'm not sure whether it was Lefèvre's fine storytelling or Livermore's larger-than-life character, but after reading that book I was hooked. I wanted to be a trader. I also believed that I could be a great trader, that I *would* be a great trader. I carried that confidence into the interview with Rich and Bill as only a 19-year old could.

Analyzing trading systems turned out to be excellent preparatory work for both the interview and the training sessions that would follow. I believe that background was one of the reasons why I took to Rich and Bill's methods faster and more confidently than the other trainees and ultimately was able to make more money for Rich than any of the other Turtles. From the very start, I had more confidence in both their approach and the concept of trading systematically than did any of the others.

That confidence played an important role in Rich's faith in my eventual success as well as in my ability to reach my trading potential. My background enabled me to do what none of the other Turtles could: follow the simple rules outlined in our two-week training class. The fact that none of the other Turtles followed those rules that first month may seem strange, but I'll save that story for later.

I was concerned at first that I might be at a disadvantage because I had not actually traded before. I believed my system-testing background might provide enough of an edge to counteract that, but my lack of experience was a primary concern. It was clear from the questions Rich and Bill asked that the candidates were being interviewed to assess our raw intellect and reasoning abilities. That did not surprise me, since one of the questions on the preinterview questionnaire had been about our SAT scores, and there had been many other questions that sought to assess our mental capacity. What did surprise me was that they were as interested in what I *did not believe* as in what I *did believe* as it related to trading.

I remember the actual moment during the interview when I became convinced that I was going to get an offer. We were discussing my disbelief at how many people were sure that there was some secret philosopher's stone that would allow one to predict the markets with uncanny accuracy. I thought that there were far too many variables involved in something as complex as the price of wheat or gold for any kind of real prediction and that the people looking for the philosopher's stone were going to be disappointed.

As an example, I recounted a story George had told me about a glass disk with many curved and straight lines on it that one could lay on a chart so that the top and bottom of the price chart would magically hit the lines as if the markets were responding to some secret order. They seemed to respond well to the story, and at that point I thought, "I'm going to get the position."

I was right—about a few things. I did get the spot, and Rich and Bill *were* testing for intelligence and aptitude. They wanted people who shared the traits they believed were necessary for profitable trading. They were also being good scientists, experimenting by intentionally building diversity into what would become known as the Turtle Class. Members of the first class included, among others, the following:

- A man who had a strong interest in gaming and games in general. He also happened to be the editor of the *Dungeon Master's Manual* for the role-playing game Dungeons and Dragons, which was all the rage in the early 1980s.

- A man with a Ph.D. in linguistics from the University of Chicago.

- A man who traded grains for Cargill and had been the Massachusetts state chess champion while in school.

- A few people with trading backgrounds.

- An accountant.

- A professional blackjack and backgammon player.

Many of these individuals were among the brightest I had ever met. Rich and Bill definitely had been screening for high intelligence, with a particular emphasis on mathematical and analytical abilities. Rich subsequently said in an interview that they were looking for "extreme intelligence," since they had so many applicants and could afford to be picky. This characteristic described many, but not all, of the Turtles. Surprisingly, I don't think that our intelligence necessarily correlated with our eventual success or failure. Another common thread was a background in gaming theory and strategy, and a good knowledge of probability mathematics as it related to games of chance. It soon would become clear why they considered this experience relevant.

A few weeks after my interview, I received a phone call from Rich telling me that I had been accepted into the training program. I must not have appeared very excited because he later told me that I was the only one of the accepted trainees who did not seem overwhelmed by the news. He wasn't even sure that I would show up for the class.

Rich told me that the training would be held during the last two weeks of the year and that after this two-week session, we would begin trading a small account. He also said that if we did well for an initial trial period with that small account, he would give us each a $1 million trading account.

It may surprise some people that Rich thought he could teach a group of traders in only two weeks. What surprises me now is that he thought it would take that long. In fact, in the second year Rich and Bill hired a new crop of Turtles and trained them in only *one* week. The difficulty in trading lies not in the concepts but in the application. It is relatively easy to learn what to do when trading. It is very difficult to apply those lessons in actual trading.

At the end of the trial trading period, which lasted one month, Rich evaluated our performance. Some Turtles received the full $1 million to trade, others were given smaller accounts, and still others were told to keep trading with the original account size. Rich gave me a $2 million account, and for the duration of the Turtle program I continued to trade the largest account for him.

In this book I will give you some of the reasons why after only one month Rich was able to assess our relative abilities, what it was he was looking for; and why he gave me a much larger account than he gave the other Turtles. Rich found this ability early on in me and eventually in many of the others; it's what I call the Way of the Turtle.

Before we get into the specifics of the Turtle Way, let me put things in context by discussing trading in general terms; and provide some insight on the psychological reasons why the Turtles were so profitable and why good traders are able to make money. The next two chapters provide a foundation for Chapter Three where we will return to the Turtle story and then dive into the details of the Turtle Way.

RISK JUNKIES

High risk, high reward: It takes balls of steel to play this game.
—Told to a friend before starting the Turtle program

People often wonder what it is that makes someone a trader rather than an investor. The distinction is often unclear because the actions of many people who call themselves investors are actually those of traders.

Investors are people who buy things for the long haul with the idea that over a considerable period—many years—their investments will appreciate in value. They buy things: actual stuff. Warren Buffett is an investor. He buys companies. He doesn't buy stock. He buys what the stock represents: the company itself, with its management team, products, and market presence. He doesn't care that the stock market may not reflect the "correct" price for his companies. In fact, he relies on that to make his money. He buys companies when they are worth much more to him than the price at which the stock market values them and sells companies when they are worth much less to him than the price at which the stock market values them. He makes a lot of money doing this because he's very good at it.

Traders do not buy physical things such as companies; they do not buy grains, gold, or silver. They buy stocks, futures contracts, and options. They do not care much about the quality of the management team, the outlook for oil consumption in the frigid Northeast, or global coffee production. Traders care about price; essentially they buy and sell *risk*.

In his informative and engaging book *Against the Gods: The Remarkable Story of Risk*, Peter Bernstein discusses how markets developed to allow the transfer of risk from one party to another. This is indeed the reason financial markets were created and a function they continue to serve.

In today's modern markets, companies can buy forward or futures contracts for currencies that will insulate their business from the effects of fluctuations in currency prices on their foreign suppliers. Companies also can buy contracts to protect themselves from future increases in the price of raw materials such as oil, copper, and aluminum.

The act of buying or selling futures contracts to offset business risks caused by price changes in raw materials or fluctuations in foreign currency exchange rates is known as *hedging*. Proper hedging can make an enormous difference for companies that are sensitive to the costs of raw goods such as oil. The airline industry, for example, is very sensitive to the cost of aviation fuel, which is tied to the price of oil. When the price of oil rises, profits drop unless ticket prices are raised. Raising ticket prices may lower sales of tickets and thus profits. Keeping ticket prices the same will lower profits as costs rise because of oil price increases.

The solution is to hedge in the oil markets. Southwest Airlines had been doing that for years, and when oil prices rose from $25 per barrel to more than $60, its costs did not increase substantially.

In fact, it was so well hedged that even years after prices started to go up, it was getting 85 percent of its oil at $26 per barrel.

It is no coincidence that Southwest Airlines has been one of the most profitable airlines over the last several years. Southwest's executives realized that their business was to fly people from place to place, not to worry about the price of oil. They used the financial markets to insulate their bottom line from the effects of oil price fluctuations. They were smart.

Who sells futures contracts to companies like Southwest that want to hedge their business risk? Traders do.

Traders Trade Risk

Traders deal in risk. There are many types of risk, and for each type of risk there is a corresponding type of trader. For the purposes of this book, we divide all those smaller risk categories into two major groups: liquidity risk and price risk.

Many traders—perhaps most of them—are very short-term operators who trade in what is known as *liquidity risk*. This refers to the risk that a trader will not be able to buy or sell: There is no buyer when you want to sell an asset or no seller when you want to buy an asset. Most people are familiar with the term *liquidity* as it applies to finance in the context of the term *liquid assets*. Liquid assets are assets that can be turned into cash readily and quickly. Cash in the bank is extremely liquid, stock in a widely traded company is relatively liquid, and a piece of land is illiquid.

Suppose that you want to buy stock XYZ and that XYZ last traded at $28.50. If you look for a price quote for XYZ, you will see two prices: the bid and the ask. For this example, let's say you get a quote on XYZ as $28.50 bid and $28.55 ask. This quote indicates that if you wanted to buy, you would have to pay $28.55, but if you wanted to sell, you would get only $28.50 for your XYZ stock. The difference between these two prices is known as the *spread*. Traders who trade liquidity risk often are referred to as *scalpers* or *market makers*. They make their money off the spread.

A variant of this kind of trading is called *arbitrage*. This entails trading the liquidity of one market for the liquidity of another. Arbitrage traders may buy crude oil in London and sell crude oil in New York, or they may buy a basket of stocks and sell index futures that represent a similar basket of stocks.

Price risk refers to the possibility that prices will move significantly up or down. A farmer would be concerned about rising oil prices because the cost of fertilizer and fuel for tractors would increase. Farmers also worry that prices for their produce (wheat, corn, soybeans, etc.) may drop so low that they will not make a profit when they sell their crops. Airline management is concerned that the cost of oil may rise and interest rates may go up, raising airplane financing costs.

Hedgers focus on getting rid of price risk by transferring the risk to traders who deal in price risk. Traders who jump on price risk are known as *speculators* or *position traders*. Speculators make money by buying and then selling later if the price goes up or by selling first and then buying back later when the price goes down—what is known as *going short*.

Traders, Speculators, and Scalpers—Oh, My

Markets are groups of traders that interact to buy and sell. Some of the traders are short-term scalpers who are only trying to make the tiny spread between bid and ask over and over again; others are speculators who are trying to profit from changes in prices; yet others are companies trying to hedge their risks. Each category is rife with experienced traders who know their jobs well, along with novices. Let's examine a set of trades to illustrate how different traders operate.

ACME Corporation is trying to hedge the risk of rising costs at its British research laboratory by buying 10 contracts of British pounds on the Chicago Mercantile Exchange (CME). ACME is at risk because the British pound has been rising and costs at the research laboratory are paid in British pounds. A rise in the exchange rate between the British pound and the dollar will increase the costs for its research facility. Hedging that risk by purchasing 10 British pound contracts will protect it from a rise in the exchange rate because the profits on the futures contracts will offset the increased costs that result from the change in the exchange rate that occurs when the British pound rises against the dollar. ACME buys the contracts for $1.8452 from a Chicago floor trader, Sam, who trades as a scalper.

The actual transaction is executed by ACME's broker, MAN Financial, which has employees on the floor. Some of those employees are phone clerks at a bank of desks that surround the trading floor, and others are traders in the British pound trading pits who execute trades for MAN. Runners take the orders from the phone desk to the trader in the pits, where that trader executes the trade with Sam. For large orders or during fast markets, the trader representing MAN on the floor may use hand signals to receive buy and sell orders from MAN's phone clerks.

Futures contracts are defined by the exchange on which they are traded in a document known as a *contract specification*. These documents define the quantity, the type of goods, and in some cases the quality of a particular commodity. In the past, the size of a contract was based on the quantity that would fit into a single railroad car: 5,000 bushels for grains, 112,000 pounds for sugar, 1,000 barrels for oil, and so on. For this reason, contracts sometimes are referred to as *cars*.

Trading takes place in units of a single contract: You cannot buy or sell less than one contract. The exchange's contract specification also defines the minimum price fluctuation. This is referred to in the industry as a *tick* or *minimum tick*.

A contract for British pounds is defined by the CME to be 62,500 British pounds, and the minimum tick is a hundredth of a cent, or $0.0001. Thus, each tick of price movement is worth $6.25. This means that Sam stands to make $62.50 for every tick in the spread because he sold 10 contracts. Since the spread at the time he sold the contracts to ACME was two ticks wide at $1.8450 bid and $1.8452 ask, Sam will try to buy 10 contracts at the other side of the spread at $1.8450 immediately. If he buys successfully at $1.8450, this will represent a profit of two ticks, or just over $100. Sam buys his 10 contracts from a large speculator, Mr. Ice, who is trying to accumulate a position betting on the price going down; this is known as a *short* position. Mr. Ice may hold those contracts for 10 days or 10 months, depending on how the market moves after this purchase.

So, there are three types of traders involved in this transaction:

- **The hedger:** ACME Corporation's trader in the hedging department, who wants to eliminate the price risk of currency fluctuation and hedges by offsetting that risk in the market

- **The scalper:** Sam, the floor trader, who trades liquidity risk and quickly trades with the hedger, hoping to earn the spread
- **The speculator:** Mr. Ice, who ultimately assumes the original "price risk" that ACME is trying to eliminate and is betting that the price will go down over the next few days or weeks

Panic in the Pits

Let's change the scenario slightly to illustrate the mechanisms behind price movement. Imagine that before Sam is able to unload his 10 contract short position by purchasing them back, a broker who works for Calyon Financial starts buying up contracts at the $1.8452 ask price. That broker purchases so many contracts that all the floor traders start to get nervous.

Although some of the floor traders may have long positions, many of them already may be short 10, 20, or even 100 contracts; this means that they will lose money if the price goes up. Since Calyon represents many large speculators and hedge funds, its buying activity is particularly worrisome. "How many more contracts is Calyon trying to buy?" the floor scalpers ask. "Who is behind the order?" "Is this just a small part of a much larger order?"

If you were a floor trader who already had sold 20 contracts short, you might be getting nervous. Suppose Calyon was trying to buy 500 or 1,000 contracts. That might bring the price up as high as $1.8460 or $1.8470. You definitely would not want to sell any more contracts at $1.8452. You might be willing to sell some at $1.8453 or $1.8455, but maybe you would be looking to get out of your contracts by buying them back at $1.8452 or perhaps even at a small loss at $1.8453 or $1.8454 instead of the $1.8450 you originally were looking for.

In a case like this, the bid–ask spread might widen to $1.8450 bid and $1.8455 ask. Or the bid and the ask might both move up, reaching $1.8452 bid and $1.8455 ask, as the scalpers who had been selling short at $1.8452 started trying to get rid of their position at the same price.

What changed? Why did the price move up? Price movement is a function of the collective perception of buyers and sellers in a market: those who are scalping to make a few ticks many times each day, those who are speculating for small moves during the day, those who are speculating for large moves over the course of weeks or months, and those who are hedging their business risks.

When the collective perception changes, the price moves. If, for whatever reason, sellers no longer are willing to sell at the current price but demand a higher price and buyers are willing to pay that higher price, the price moves up. If, for whatever reason, buyers no longer are willing to pay the current price but only a lower price and there are sellers who are willing to sell at that lower price, the price goes down.

The collective perception can take on a life of its own. If enough floor traders are caught with short positions when a large buy order comes in, panic can ensue. A large buyer might drive the price up sufficiently to trigger other buy orders that have been placed in the markets, causing even more price movement. For this reason, experienced scalpers will get out of their short positions quickly and scalp only on the buying side when prices start moving up.

Using the example described above, a floor trader who is not quick enough might rapidly find himself with a 10-, 20-, or even 50-tick loss per contract. If he holds 50 contracts with a 50-tick loss, this represents a loss of $15,625 (50 × 50 × $6.25), more money than he may have made that entire week or month. At some point the psychological pain of watching so much money disappear may be so great that the floor scalper panics and buys at whatever price the market offers. In a fast market this may take only 1 or 2 minutes; in a slower market it may take 10 or 15.

One can see that the experienced trader not only buys out of her short position early, she buys a few more contracts to profit further as the price moves up. When a less experienced trader panics and starts buying, an opportunity is presented to an experienced trader to again sell and exit his recently acquired long position to make another profit.

Death of the Pits

When we traded as Turtles, futures contracts were bought and sold exclusively in trading pits at the commodity exchanges, where men fought mano a mano to execute their trades with other traders using hand signals and shouting. To outsiders it looked like insanity at times.

The pits are dying. Electronic exchanges are replacing them in almost every market. Among other benefits, the costs for electronic execution are lower, the executions are quicker, and traders can determine if they are filled in milliseconds instead of minutes. These advantages are killing the pit traded futures. In every market where electronic trading and pit trading coexist, the volume has moved to the electronic markets. In fact, it is likely that before this book goes out of print there will no longer be U.S. exchanges where futures contracts are traded in pits.

Those of us who have been involved in trading since before the advent of electronic exchanges are saddened by the death of the pits. In Chicago, there are many examples of traders like Richard Dennis who came from a working-class background and made their millions trading in the pits. For those who are skillful, the pits are better places to trade. In the pits you can see the psychology of the market in the faces of the other traders. Numbers on a screen just don't convey the same kind of information. Many traders had their start running orders into the pit from the banks of phones that surrounded them. These jobs are disappearing.

Nevertheless, while we are saddened and nostalgic about the pits, the new electronic markets offer some new opportunities. Execution costs are lower, and this creates opportunities to trade using strategies that trade more frequently. Some of the electronic markets have such large volume that it is possible to buy and sell millions of dollars worth of futures contracts without even beginning to move the price.

Keep in mind that when I refer to traders in this book as executing trades in pits, this may not be the way trading is currently transacted in many markets. The players and actions, however, are still the same. The pain of a losing trade is still present whether you trade electronically or you call a broker on the phone and the trade is transacted in the pits. The hedgers, scalpers, and speculators are still there, hiding behind the screen—waiting to eat you alive if you let them.

The next chapter delves into the psychological biases that create differences in outlook and behavior between an inexperienced and probably losing trader and his more successful and experienced counterpart. It also discusses the different types of trading styles and market states that favor each of those styles. Later chapters show how Rich's training turned very inexperienced traders into profitable ones in only a few weeks time.

TAMING THE
TURTLE MIND

*Human emotion is both the source of opportunity in trading
and the greatest challenge. Master it and you will succeed.
Ignore it at your peril.*

To trade well you need to understand the human mind. Markets are comprised of individuals, all with hopes, fears and foibles. As a trader you are seeking out opportunities that arise from these human emotions. Fortunately, some very smart people—behavioral finance pioneers—have identified the ways that human emotion affects one's decision-making process. The field of behavioral finance—brought to popular attention in Robert Shiller's fascinating book, now in its Second Edition, titled *Irrational Exuberance* and greater details of which were published by Hersh Shefrin in his classic *Beyond Greed and Fear*—helps traders and investors understand the reasons why markets operate the way they do.

Just what does make prices go up and down? (Price movements can turn an otherwise stoic individual into a blubbering pile of misery.) Behavioral finance is able to explain market phenomena and price action by focusing on the cognitive and psychological factors that affect buying and selling decisions. The approach has shown that people are prone to making systematic errors in circumstances of uncertainty. Under duress, people make poor assessments of risk and event probabilities. What could be more stressful than winning or losing money? Behavioral finance has proved that when it comes to such scenarios, people rarely make completely rational decisions. Successful traders understand this tendency and benefit from it. They know that someone else's errors in judgment are opportunities, and good traders understand how those errors manifest themselves in market price action: The Turtles knew this.

Emotional Rescue

For many years economic and financial theory was based on the *rational actor* theory, which stated that individuals act rationally and consider all available information in the decision-making process. Traders have always known that this notion is pure bunk. Winning traders make money by exploiting the consistently irrational behavior patterns of other traders. Academic researchers have uncovered a surprisingly large amount of evidence demonstrating that most individuals do not act rationally. Dozens of categories of irrational behavior and repeated errors in judgment have been documented in academic studies. Traders find it very puzzling that anyone ever thought otherwise.

The Turtle Way works and continues to work because it is based on the *market movements that result from the systematic and repeated irrationality that is embedded in every person.*

How many times have you felt these emotions while trading?

- **Hope:** I sure hope this goes up right after I buy it.
- **Fear:** I can't take another loss; I'll sit this one out.
- **Greed:** I'm making so much money, I'm going to double my position.
- **Despair:** This trading system doesn't work; I keep losing money.

With the Turtle Way, market actions are identified that indicate opportunities arising from these consistent human traits. This chapter examines specific examples of how human emotion and irrational thinking create repetitive market patterns that signal moneymaking opportunities.

People have developed certain ways of looking at the world that served them well in more primitive circumstances; however, when it comes to trading, those perceptions get in the way. Scientists call distortions in the way people perceive reality *cognitive biases*. Here are some of the cognitive biases that affect trading:

- **Loss aversion:** The tendency for people to have a strong preference for avoiding losses over acquiring gains
- **Sunk costs effect:** The tendency to treat money that already has been committed or spent as more valuable than money that may be spent in the future
- **Disposition effect:** The tendency for people to lock in gains and ride losses
- **Outcome bias:** The tendency to judge a decision by its outcome rather than by the quality of the decision at the time it was made

- **Recency bias:** The tendency to weigh recent data or experience more than earlier data or experience
- **Anchoring:** The tendency to rely too heavily, or anchor, on readily available information
- **Bandwagon effect:** The tendency to believe things because many other people believe them
- **Belief in the law of small numbers:** The tendency to draw unjustified conclusions from too little information

Although this list is not comprehensive, it includes some of the most powerful misperceptions that affect trading and prices. Let's look at each cognitive bias in greater detail.

People who are affected by *loss aversion* have an absolute preference for avoiding losses rather than acquiring gains. For most people, losing $100 is not the same as not winning $100. However, from a rational point of view the two things are the same: They both represent a net negative change of $100. Research has suggested that losses can have as much as twice the psychological power of gains.

In terms of trading, loss aversion affects one's ability to follow mechanical trading systems because the losses incurred in following a system are felt more strongly than are the potential winnings from using that system. People feel the pain of losing much more strongly when they follow rules than they do when they incur the same losses from a missed opportunity or by ignoring the rules of the system. Thus, a $10,000 loss is felt as strongly as a $20,000 missed opportunity.

In business, *sunk costs* are costs that already have been incurred and cannot be recovered. For example, an investment that already has been spent on research for a new technology is a sunk cost. The *sunk cost effect* is the tendency for people to consider the amount of money that already has been spent—the sunk costs—when making decisions.

Say the ACME Company has spent $100 million developing a particular technology for building laptop displays. Now suppose that after spending this money it becomes obvious that an alternative technology is much better and more likely to produce the desired results in the required time frame. A purely rational approach would be to weigh the future costs of adopting the new technology against the future expense of continuing to use the developed technology and then make a decision solely on the basis of future benefits and expenditures, completely disregarding the amount of money that already has been spent.

However, the sunk cost effect causes those who make this decision to consider the amount of money previously spent and view it as a waste of $100 million if a different technology is used. They may choose to continue with the original decision even if it means spending two or three times as much in the future to build the laptop displays. The sunk cost effect leads to bad decision making that often is heightened in group situations.

How does this phenomenon influence trading? Consider the typical new trader who initiated a trade with the expectation of winning $2,000. At the time the trade first was entered, he decided that he would exit the position if the price dropped to the point where a $1,000 loss would be incurred. After a few days, the trade's position is at a $500 loss. A few more days pass and the loss grows to over $1,000: More than 10 percent of the trading account. The value of that account has dropped from $10,000 to less than $9,000.

This also happens to be the point where the trader previously decided to exit.

Consider how cognitive biases might affect the decision whether to keep true to the prior commitment to get out at a $1,000 loss or to keep holding the position. Loss aversion makes it extremely painful for the trader to consider exiting the position because that would make the loss permanent. As long as he does not exit, he believes there is a chance that the market will come back and turn the loss into a win. The sunk cost effect makes the decision not one of deciding what the market is likely to do in the future but one of finding ways to avoid wasting the $1,000 that already has been spent on the trade. So, the new trader continues to hold the position not because of what he believes the market is likely to do but because he does not want to take a loss *and* waste that $1,000. What will he do when the price drops even more and the loss increases to $2,000?

Rational thought dictates that he will exit. Regardless of his earlier assumption about the market, the market clearly is telling him that he was wrong, since it is far past the point at which he originally decided to exit. Unfortunately, both biases are even stronger at this point. The loss he wishes to avoid is now larger and even more painful to consider. For many, this kind of behavior will continue until the trader loses all his money or finally panics and exits with a loss of 30 to 50 percent of his account, perhaps three to five times what he had planned.

I worked in Silicon Valley during the height of the Internet craze and had many friends who were engineers and marketers for high-tech companies. Several of them were worth millions from stock options on companies that recently had gone public. They watched the prices go up day after day during late 1999 and early 2000. As prices started to drop in 2000, I asked many of them when they were going to sell their stock. The reply was inevitably something along the lines of the following: "I'll sell if it gets back up to $X," a price that was significantly higher than the level at which the market was when I asked. Almost every single one of my friends who was in this position watched the price of his or her stock drop to a tenth or even a hundredth of its previous value without selling the shares. The lower it dropped, the easier it was for them to justify waiting. "Well I've already lost $2 million. What's a few more hundred thousand?" they would say.

The *disposition effect* is the tendency for investors to sell shares whose price is increasing and keep shares that have dropped in value. Some say that this effect is related to the sunk cost effect since both provide evidence of people not wanting to face the reality of a prior decision that has not worked out. Similarly, the tendency to lock in winning trades stems from the desire to avoid losing the winnings. For traders who exhibit this tendency, it becomes very difficult to make up for large losses when winning trades are prematurely cut short of their potential.

Outcome bias is the propensity to judge a decision by its outcome rather than by the quality of the decision at the time it was made. Much of life is uncertain. There are no right answers to many of the questions that involve risk and uncertainty. For this reason, a person sometimes will make a decision that he considers rational and that appears to be correct, but as a result of unforeseen and unforeseeable circumstances that decision will not lead to the desired outcome.

Outcome bias causes people to put too much emphasis on what actually occurred rather than on the quality of the decision itself. In trading, even a correct approach can result in losing trades, perhaps a few in a row. These losses can cause traders to doubt themselves and their decision process, and they then evaluate the approach they have been using negatively because the outcome of that approach has been negative. The next bias makes this problem particularly acute.

Recency bias is the tendency for individuals to place greater importance on more recent data and experience. A trade that was made yesterday weighs more heavily than do trades from last week or last year. Two months of losing trades can count as much as or more than the six months of winning trades that happened previously. Thus, the outcome of a series of recent trades will cause most traders to doubt their method and decision-making process.

Anchoring is the tendency for people to rely too heavily on readily available information when making a decision involving uncertainty. They may anchor a recent price and make decisions on the basis of how the current price relates to that price. This is one of the reasons my friends had such difficulty selling their stocks: They were anchoring on the recent highs and comparing the current price with those highs. After they made that comparison, the current price always looked too low.

The observation that people often believe things because many other people believe them is known as the *bandwagon effect* or the *herd effect*. The bandwagon effect is partially responsible for the seemingly unstoppable increase in prices at the end of a price bubble.

People who fall under the spell of the *law of small numbers* believe that a small sample closely resembles the population from which it is drawn. The term is taken from the statistical law of large numbers, which shows that a large sample drawn from a population *does* closely resemble the population from which it is taken. This law is the basis of all polling. A sample of 500 taken randomly from a larger population can give very good estimations for a population of 200 million or more people.

In contrast, very small samples do not reveal much about the underlying population. For example, if a trading strategy works four times out of a test of six times, most people would say the strategy is a good one, whereas statistical evidence indicates that there is not enough information to draw that conclusion with any certainty. If a mutual fund manager outperforms the indexes three years in a row, he is considered a hero. Unfortunately, a few years of performance says very little about what the long-term expectations might be. Belief in the law of small numbers causes people to gain and lose too much confidence too quickly. When combined with the recency effect and outcome bias, it often results in traders abandoning valid approaches just before those approaches start working again.

Cognitive biases have a profound effect on traders because if a trader is not influenced by them, almost every bias creates opportunities to make money. In the following chapters, as specific aspects of the Turtle Way are explored, you will see how avoiding these biases can provide you with a significant advantage in trading.

The Turtle Way

Now that we've discussed the mind-set of a trader, let's look at the many ways to make money trading. Different types of trading strategies or trading styles have their aficionados. In fact, some traders believe in their particular style with such fervor that all others are considered inferior. I hold no such belief. Anything that works, works. Doggedly sticking to a method to the exclusion of all others is foolish. This section explores some of the most popular trading styles currently in use. The first approach I'll discuss is known as *trend following*.

Trend Following

In trend following, the trader attempts to capitalize on large price movements over the course of several months. Trend followers enter trades when markets are at historical highs or lows and exit when a market reverses and sustains that movement for a few weeks.

Traders spend a lot of time developing methods to determine exactly when a trend has begun and when it has ended; however, all the approaches that are effective have very similar performance characteristics. Trend following generates excellent returns and has done so consistently for as long as anyone has traded futures contracts, but it is not an easy strategy for most people to follow for several reasons.

First, large trends occur fairly infrequently; this means that trend-following strategies generally have a much higher percentage of losing trades than winning trades. It may be typical for a trend-following system to have 65 or 70 percent losing trades.

Second, in addition to losing money when there are no trends, trend-following systems lose when trends reverse. A common expression that the Turtles and other trend followers use is "The trend is your friend until the end when it bends." The bends at the end can be brutal both on your account and on your psyche.

Traders refer to these losing periods as *drawdowns*. Drawdowns usually begin after a trendy period ends, but they can continue for months when markets are choppy, and the trend-following strategies continue to generate losing trades.

Drawdowns generally are measured in terms of both their length (in days or months) and their extent (usually in percentage terms). As a general rule, one can expect drawdowns for trend-following systems to approach the level of the returns. Thus, if a trend-following system is expected to generate a 30 percent annual return, you can expect a losing period in which the account may drop 30 percent from its highs.

Third, trend following requires a relatively large amount of money to trade using reasonable risk limits because of the large distance between the entry price and the stop loss price at which one would exit if the trade did not work out.

Trading with a trend-following strategy with too little money greatly increases the odds of going bust. We will examine this problem in much greater detail in Chapter 8, "Risk and Money Management."

Countertrend Trading

A countertrend trading style makes money when markets are not trending by using a strategy that is the opposite of trend following. Instead of buying when markets make new highs, traders who use countertrend strategies sell short at prices close to the same new highs, counting on the fact that most breakouts of new highs do not result in trends. In Chapter 6 we will look at the market mechanisms that are the source of profit for countertrend trading: support and resistance.

Swing Trading

Swing trading is essentially the same as trend following except that it targets shorter-term market moves. For example, a good swing trade may last three or four days instead of several months. Swing traders often look for patterns in price movement that indicate a higher likelihood of a significant short-term price movement in one direction or another.

Swing traders tend to use shorter-term charts that show price bars for every five minutes, fifteen minutes, or every hour. On these charts a large three- or four-day move will appear the way a three- to six-month trend does on a daily bar chart.

Day Trading

Day trading is not so much a style as it is a reference to the extremely short-term time frames involved. A true day trader looks to exit the market before it closes each day. This makes his or her position less susceptible to large adverse moves spurred by news occurring overnight. Day traders generally use one of three different trading styles: position trading, scalping, or arbitrage.

Day traders generally use a style such as trend following or countertrend trading but do it over a much shorter period. A trade may last a few hours instead of days or months.

Scalping is a specialized form of trading that was once the domain of only those traders on the floor of the exchange. Scalpers are looking to make the difference between the bid and the ask, which is known as the *spread*. If gold is $550 bid and $551 ask, a scalper will be looking to buy at $550 and sell at $551. For this reason scalpers create liquidity by bidding and offering, hoping for a balance of buy and sell orders.

Arbitrage is a form of trading that capitalizes on price differences in the same market or in very similar markets. Often these markets are traded on different exchanges. For example, an arbitrage trader may buy gold on the Comex floor at $550 and sell five e-mini gold contracts on the CBOT's globex exchange for $555 to capture a very short-term price mismatch.

Watching the Market State

Each of these strategies tends to work better some of the time: When the price movement of a market behaves in a particular way or when that market is in a particular state.

As Figure 2-1 illustrates, speculative markets exist in one of four states:

- **Stable and quiet:** Prices tend to stay within a relatively small range with little movement up or down outside that range.
- **Stable and volatile:** There are large daily or weekly changes, but without major changes over a period of months.
- **Trending and quiet:** There is slow movement or drift in prices when measured over a period of months but without severe retracement or price movement in the opposite direction.
- **Trending and volatile:** There are large changes in price accompanied by occasional significant shorter-term reversals of direction.

Trend followers love markets that are trending and quiet. They can make money without having significant adverse price movement.

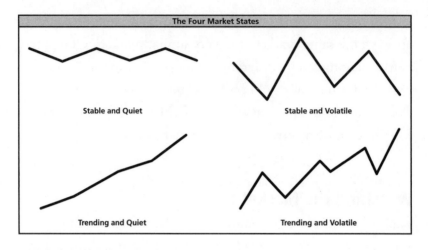

Figure 2-1 The Four Market States

This makes it very easy to keep a trade for a long time because the market does not give back profits during the trade. Volatile markets are much more punishing for trend followers. It can be very difficult to hold onto a trade when profits are vanishing for days or weeks at a time.

Countertrend traders love markets that are stable and volatile. These types of markets have relatively large swings but remain in a fairly narrow range of prices. Swing traders like volatile markets, whether trending or not. Volatile markets present more opportunities because swing traders make money on short term price moves. These types of moves are the characteristic that defines volatile markets.

Although it's sometimes easy to tell when a market is in one of these states, both the degree of trendiness and the volatility vary over time. This means that many times markets simultaneously display characteristics of two states, with one of the attributes shifting from a low value to a high one or vice versa. For instance, you may have a market that starts out trending and quiet, and then as the trend progresses, the volatility increases so that you get price movement that changes from trending and quiet to trending and volatile.

A Turtle never tries to predict market direction but instead *looks for indications that a market is in a particular state*. This is an important concept. Good traders don't try to predict what the market *will do*; instead they look at the indications of what the market *is doing*.

STEP 1   STATE

THE FIRST $2 MILLION
IS THE TOUGHEST

Trade with an edge, manage risk, be consistent, and keep it simple.
The entire Turtle training, and indeed the basis for all successful
trading, can be summed up in these four core principles.

The Turtle training sessions were held in a conference room at the Union League Club in Chicago, two blocks east of the CBOT. From the get-go, the experience was rife with contradiction. For instance, we were instructed to wear jackets since the Union League Club had a dress code, but that did not mesh with Rich's personality. He was not the kind of guy who would require a dress code. Also, I have no idea how we ended up in this particular room, but one could not have chosen a more unlikely place for our training. The Union League Club was the quintessential gentleman's club. Its early members included such Chicago luminaries as Philip Danforth Armour of the meat company; George Pullman, who created the luxury Pullman railroad car; Marshall Field; and John Deere. Picture a room filled with cigar smoke and you'll have a pretty good feel for the Union

League Club in 1983. It was worlds away from the subdued offices at C&D Commodities.

Thirteen of us made up the first Turtle class: eleven men and two women. Many of those in attendance already had experience trading, but several of us were complete novices. I was considerably younger than my classmates. There were a couple of trainees who looked to be in their mid-twenties, but most were in their thirties as far as I could tell. Even though I was only 19, I felt as though I were among a group of peers; the age and experience of the others did not intimidate me.

Before getting into the particulars of what we were taught, let me describe a few things about myself to help you understand how my personality and perspectives influenced what I took away from Rich's class. I like to simplify concepts and am adept at getting to the core of a matter—to its essence. Throughout the sessions, I did not need to take detailed notes on what was said; I listened for the most important concepts: the key ideas. I paid attention to what was being said and why it was being said. I firmly believe that my strong performance during the first month of trading was due to this ability and to identifying the most important of Rich's lessons.

Class Begins

Both Rich and Bill taught the class, and their innovative perspectives struck me from the beginning. They approached the markets scientifically and through the use of reason, and developed a very mature understanding of the principles behind their success. Rich and Bill did not rely on gut feelings. Instead, they based their methods on experimentation and investigation. They did not use anecdotal evidence but relied on computerized analysis to determine what worked and what did not. Their intensive scientific research gave them a special type of confidence in thinking about trading that has been crucial to their success. (This is what had given Rich the confidence required to stake his money on being able to teach a group of neophytes to trade in the first place.)

Rich and Bill first taught us the foundations of basic gaming and probability theory. I had taken probability and statistics in high school, so that material was not new to me. They explained to us the mathematical basis for money management, risk of ruin, and expectation—all of which are well-known gambling concepts. Several of the Turtles had been former professional gamblers, and so they were already familiar with these basics. I'll explore these theories more thoroughly in later chapters, but here I'll give you a brief synopsis of what was covered in the class.

Risk of Ruin

Searching for the term *risk of ruin* on the Internet will yield many references to gambling and blackjack because the concept is much more popular in gambling than in trading. However, risk of ruin is a trader's primary consideration in deciding how many contracts of a particular market or shares of a particular stock to trade at any specific time.

In gambling, risk of ruin refers to the possibility that you will drop all your money because of a string of losses. For example, suppose we were rolling dice and I said I would give you $2 for every $1 you bet if a roll of a single die came up with a 4, 5, or 6. You would want to bet as much as possible, since these are

great odds. The chances that a 4, 5, or 6 will come up is 50 percent, since there are six sides, and three of those sides will pay 2
to 1. The odds indicate that if you rolled four times, you most
likely would get two losses and two wins. If you bet $100 each
time, you'd lose twice and win twice for a net gain of $200 for
the four rolls.

What size bet would you make if you had only $1,000 in your
pocket: $1,000? $500? $100? The problem is that even though the
game is in your favor, you still have a chance of losing. If you bet too
big and lose too many times in a row, you could lose all your money
and forfeit the ability to keep playing through pure chance. If you
bet $500 and lose twice in a row, you'll be out of money. There is a
25 percent chance of losing twice in a row on the first two rolls; so
with a $500 bet, your risk of ruin is 25 percent with just two rolls.

One of the most important aspects of risk of ruin is that it
increases disproportionately as the size of the bet rises. Doubling
the amount risked per trade typically will not just double the risk
of ruin; depending on the particulars of the system, it might triple,
quadruple, or even quintuple it.

The Science of Controlled Risk

Money management refers to managing the size of market risk
to ensure one's ability to keep going through the inevitable bad
periods that every trader experiences. Money management is the
science of keeping your risk of ruin at acceptable levels while
maximizing your profit potential.

The Turtles used two approaches to money management. First,
we put our positions in small chunks. That way, in the event of a

losing trade we would have a loss on only a portion of a position. Rich and Bill called those chunks *units*. Second, we used an innovative method they devised for determining the position size for each market. The method is based on the daily movement of the market either upward or downward in constant dollar terms. They determined the number of contracts in each market that would cause them *all* to move up and down by approximately the same dollar amount. Rich and Bill called the volatility measure N, although it now is known more commonly as *average true range*. That is the name given to it by J. Welles Wilder in his book *New Concepts in Technical Trading Systems*.

Since the number of contracts we traded in each market was adjusted for the volatility measure, N, the daily fluctuations for any specific trade tended to be similar. The concept of adjusting trade size on the basis of volatility (position size) has been written about by others, most notably by Van Tharp in his 1998 book *Trade Your Way to Financial Freedom* and the second edition of that book, published in 2007. However, in 1983 this was an extremely innovative concept. At that time most traders adjusted their position sizes in various markets on the basis of loose subjective criteria or the broker's *margin* requirements, which were based only loosely on volatility.

The Turtle Edge

Since several of us did not have any trading experience, significant time was spent on the mechanics of order entry and trading. Rich and Bill also covered several concepts that were important even for experienced traders to review since few in the class had traded accounts as large as Rich proposed giving us. Trading large accounts presents its own difficulties because the size of the orders can cause the markets to move, making it more expensive to trade. Effectively managing orders is important in minimizing this effect.

The Turtles were taught to use limit orders rather than market orders, which we did most of the time. Large market orders invariably move the price. A limit order, sometimes known as an *or better* order, is one in which you buy at a specific price or better. For example, if you want to buy gold and the price is currently at 540 and has been moving between 538 and 542 for the last 10 minutes, you might put in an order to buy at "539 limit" or "539 or better." In this scenario, if you had placed a market order, it most likely would have been filled at the higher price of 541 or 542. Over time, even small differences in price add up to a lot of money.

Arguably the most important element of the Turtle Way and the pivotal difference between the approach and perspective used by winning traders and that used by losing traders is that the Turtles *were taught how to think in terms of the long run when trading and we were given a system with an **edge***.

Trading methods that work over the long run have what is known in gambling as an *edge*. An edge refers to one's systematic advantage over an opponent. Most of the time casinos have the edge over their clientele. With some games it is possible for players to gain an edge. Skillful blackjack card counters are able to gain a temporary edge over the house when they notice that a large number of low cards have been played. This means that there is a higher possibility that any card draw from the deck will be a high card. During these times, the players can have an advantage over the house. They have a temporary edge. This is because the house must hit on any combination of cards up to 16. If there are a large number of high cards remaining in the deck, that means that there is a higher possibility that one of these cards will cause the house to go bust, since any combination of cards over 21 points will cause the house to lose.

So a skillful card player plays with small bets during the majority of the time when the house has an edge. They lie in wait for the occasion when due to random chance the player gains a temporary edge over the house. At these times the players bet with large bets to press their advantage over the house. In practice, this is not so easy because one sure way of getting noticed by the house and getting kicked out of the casino is to bet minimums and then suddenly bet maximums when the odds turn in your favor.

This is one of the reasons that many successful gamblers operate in teams. One team member might count at the table and then indicate to another team member when the odds had turned. That other member would show up as a new player and then proceed to bet from the start at a much higher level. Team members would then pool their money at the end of the night. These methods work because the professional gamblers have a system with an edge.

Rich and Bill taught us expectation so we would have a firm intellectual basis for being able to continue with our methods during the periods of losing trades which come when trading any strategy. The systems we were taught had a very significant edge during the markets when we traded them. Expectation was one way of quantifying that edge. It was also an intellectual foundation for avoiding the outcome bias.

Remember outcome bias: the tendency to judge a decision on the basis of its outcome rather than on the quality of that decision at the time it was made? We were trained explicitly to avoid outcome bias, to ignore the individual outcomes of particular trades and focus on expectation instead.

Expectation: Quantifying the Edge

The term *expectation* is also derived from gambling theory and answers the question "What happens if I keep doing this?" in quantifiable terms. Positive expectation games are those in which it is possible to win; the blackjack example above when the player counts cards has positive expectation. Negative expectation games are those such as roulette and craps where the house has the advantage and so over the long run a gambler will lose. Casino owners understand expectation very well. They know that games of chance in which the house has a positive expectation of even just a few percentage points can provide large sums of money over the course of multiple players and many days. Casino owners do not care about the losses they incur because such losses only encourage their gambling clientele. For owners, losses are just the cost of doing business; they know they will come out ahead over the long run.

The Turtle Mind
• Think in terms of the long run when trading.
• Avoid outcome bias.
• Believe in the effects of trading with positive expectation.

The Turtle Way views losses in the same manner: They are the cost of doing business rather than an indication of a trading error or a bad decision. To approach losses in this way, we had to know that the method by which the losses were incurred would pay out over the long run. *The Turtles believed in the long-term success of trading with positive expectation.*

Rich and Bill might say that a particular system had an expectation of 0.2; that meant that over time you would make 20¢ for every dollar risked on a particular trade. They determined the expectation for trading systems by analyzing a system's historical trades. Expectation was based on the average dollar amount won per trade divided by the average amount risked. That risk is determined by the difference between the entry price and the stop loss price (the price at which we would exit in the event of a loss), multiplied by the number of contracts traded, multiplied by the size of the contract itself.

Here's an example that illustrates how the Turtles measured risk. For a gold trade entered long at $350 with a stop at $320 for 10 contracts, there is a risk of the $30 difference between the entry price and the stop loss exit price multiplied by the position size of 10 contracts, multiplied by the size of the contract itself, which is 100 ounces. Once those numbers are multiplied, you have a total of $3,000.

The Turtles were encouraged to look at the long-term results of a specific approach and ignore the losses we expected to incur while trading with that approach. In fact, we were taught that periods of losses usually precede periods of good trading. This training was critical to both the Turtles' potential success and their ability to keep trading according to a specific set of rules through extended periods of losing trades.

Trend Following

Trends are sustained changes in price that occur over a period of weeks or months. The basic idea of trend following is to buy just as a trend toward higher prices starts and exit just after that trend ends. Markets have the inclination to move, or *trend*, in one of three directions: up, down or sideways. The Turtles were taught to buy just as the market moved from trending sideways to trending up and also to sell short just as a trend down would begin, exiting each trend after it ended, i.e. when the trend went from moving up or down to moving sideways again.

It is funny how over the years the secret rules of the Turtles have been discussed and some individuals have charged thousands of dollars to teach them. The reality is that the particular rules we used were a fairly unimportant component of our success. There are many other widely known trend-following methods that work equally well, and many that are arguably better. In fact, even the method we traded with was well known at the time we used it.

The secret of trading and of the Turtles' success is that you can trade successfully by using ideas and concepts that are well known and have been around for years. But you have to follow those rules consistently.

The specific method we used was known as the breakout, sometimes referred to as Donchian channels after Richard Donchian, who popularized the breakout method of trading. The basic idea was to buy if a market exceeded the highest price for a particular number of preceding days, that is, *broke out* of its prior price levels. We had an intermediate-length system that Rich and Bill called *System 1* that considered 20 days (or 4 trading weeks) of prices to determine the highs and lows and a longer-term system, *System 2*, that used 60-day (12-week) highs and lows to determine the break-out. We would calculate the most extreme highs and lows for each system at the end of each day. Generally, this meant looking back to determine one or two prices that were the high on the basis of their visual appearance. Most days, the highs would remain the same and there would be no work to do. Each system had two types of exits. The first was a stop loss exit that was a maximum of 2N, or two average true ranges away from the entry point. This also happened to represent 2 percent of our account because the way we determined the number of contracts to trade per market also was based on N (average true range).

The lessons of the Turtle class can be summed up in these four points:

1. **Trade with an Edge:** Find a trading strategy that will produce positive returns over the long run because it has a positive expectation.

2. **Manage Risk:** Control risk so that you can continue to trade or you may not be around to see the benefits of a positive expectation system.

3. **Be Consistent:** Execute your plan consistently to achieve the positive expectation of your system.

4. **Keep It Simple:** The core of our approach was simple: catch every trend. Two or three trades might account for all your profits, so don't miss a trend or you might kill your whole year. This is simple and easy to understand, not easy to do.

This last point is an important one, as you will see in the following section when I discuss our actual trading. The details of our specific approach were not as important in my mind when we started trading as were being consistent and not missing a trend. These simple concepts were easily missed when we started to put real money on the line.

Things Heat Up

Our two weeks of training completed, the class was eager to begin trading. We returned to Chicago after the New Year holiday, and each one of us was given a desk in a large office on the eighth floor of the Insurance Exchange building right next to the CBOT on Jackson.

The desks were arranged in pairs of six that had six-foot partitions between them. We each had the chance to choose a desk, and that meant that we selected the person we would be sitting next to for the indefinite future. Each desk had a telephone with a private line that rang directly at that desk.

The Turtles were given a sheet each week that listed the number of contracts per million in the trading account for each of the markets we traded. However, to simplify the process for the practice trades, we were told to use a fixed unit size of three contracts for each market. We were to take a position of at most 4 units or 12 contracts for each commodity we traded. That roughly corresponded to an account size of $50,000 to $100,000.

We had full discretion over our accounts and could make any trades we wanted as long as we stated the reasons behind a trade and followed the general outlines of our system. We did this by maintaining a log for the first month that indicated the reasons behind every trade we made. Most of my entries were of the following form: "Entered long at $400.00 because it was a 60-day breakout according to the rules of System 2."

A few days into the New Year, February heating oil rose from about $0.80 to $0.84, and so I followed the system and bought three contracts. The trade was immediately profitable, and in just a few days I had bought the maximum 12 contracts. Over the next several days, our "trading room" was buzzing with orders and the euphoria of quick profits: Heating oil rose to over $0.98 in less than a week.

This was before the days when computers printed charts automatically. We followed the charts printed in *Commodities Perspective*, a tabloid-sized newspaper with charts for most of the actively traded futures contracts that month. Since the charts were updated only once per week, we needed to pencil in the prices for new days after the close each day.

Heating oil challenged that approach because we were only two weeks from the end of the contract expiration, and so *Commodities Perspective* stopped covering the February contract. The problem was that we had to use our old chart, which only went up to about $0.90 since the high of the last year had been only $0.89. This meant that the price was literally "off the charts." To deal with this, I cut out a section of the previous week's charts that did not have any prices on it and taped it to the top of the chart. The prices extended about 12 inches past the top of the original chart.

While doing this, I noticed something that struck me as very odd; in fact, it still does. I was the only Turtle with a full position. Every other single Turtle had decided for some unfathomable reason *not* to follow the system Rich and Bill had outlined.

I don't know if it was fear of losing too soon after starting, the fact that the February contract of heating oil was going to expire in a few weeks, or simply a preference for a more conservative trading style, but I could not figure out how everyone could have attended the same training session I did and not be completely loaded in February heating oil. (*Loaded* was a expression we used to indicate having the maximum four-unit position.)

We were told over and over not to miss a trend, and here it was only a few weeks later and many of the Turtles had missed the boat on a very significant one. If we had been trading a normal $1 million account, we would have had a unit size of 18 contracts instead of 3, meaning that I would have made about $500,000, or 50 percent, on this trade.

The few days that followed my noticing that I was the only one who had the full position were volatile. Heating oil dropped in price from a high of about $0.98 to $0.94, or about $1,200 per contract. After the price dropped for two straight days, I noticed something else that I found interesting.

According to Rich and Bill's training, it was very clear that the right thing to do during a brief drop was to hold on and let the profits run. Therefore, that is what I did: I held all 12 contracts as the price dropped. In just a couple of days I saw my profits drop from about from $50,000 to $35,000. Upon seeing the profits evaporate, the few Turtles who had significant positions liquidated their contracts.

Then the markets woke up. The next day the price began to rise again. Soon it passed the previous high of $0.98 and kept rising to over $1.05. It reached its peak a day or two before the contract was due to expire.

I got a call from Dale in Rich's office informing me that Rich did not want to take delivery of heating oil, and so I ended up getting out of all 12 contracts at $1.03, which was very near the contract high of $1.053 for the February contract. The vast majority of the time the looming expiration date for a contract did not cause us to exit a position. Instead, we simply transferred our position into the next liquid contract by exiting the expiring month and taking a new position in the next month. In this case things were different; the trend had only taken place in the February 1984 contract, so there was no reason to roll. This also meant that I needed to stay in the February contract in order to ride the trend.

Figure 3-1 shows the February 1984 heating oil prices and the entry and exit for our first major trend as Turtles.

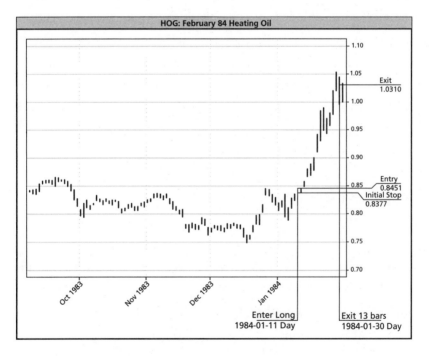

Figure 3-1 The Turtles' First Trend

After the trade was over, my account was up $78,000. I was rewarded for holding to the methods we were taught by earning almost three times as much on this trade as any of the other Turtles did. The few who had positions of a reasonable size had all exited near the lows of the previous dip and ended up missing half the move. The Turtles who had not entered the trade made nothing.

The difference in return had nothing to do with knowledge and everything to do with emotional and psychological factors. It seemed crazy to me. We all had been taught exactly the same thing, but my return for January was three times that of the others in the class or more. These were very intelligent people who had been taught by the most famous trader of that time. Several of them would be among the most successful traders in the world within a few years, yet they had failed to execute the plan during the practice trading period.

Over the years I kept finding evidence that *emotional and psychological strength are the most important ingredients in successful trading*. This was my first exposure to that idea and the first time I had seen it in action.

The First Report Card

During the first month of trading, Rich and Bill dropped by once a week or every other week. After the first month was over, they came by and conducted an extensive Q&A session with the group. In it, Rich asked all the Turtles why they had not bought more heating oil. Some answered that they had thought the trade was too risky, that it had gone up too fast; others had thought the move would not last because there were only a few days left for trading the contract.

I had looked at things differently. At the time, I based my strategy on the belief that Rich would be evaluating us on our ability to execute the systems we were taught. I also thought he would look more favorably on trades faithfully executed that incurred losses than on trades we should have taken but did not, even if that avoided losses.

I thought the riskiest thing to do was *not* take the heating oil trade. During the Q&A, Rich made it clear to everyone that taking the trade was the correct move. The scenario could not have been better for teaching the class a valuable lesson. Slightly more than one month after training, we had witnessed in actual trading the importance of not missing trends and had that lesson reinforced in such a way that none of us would ever forget it.

Rich had told us that after the first month that he would give those of us who did well a $1 million account to trade. He had indicated before we actually traded that many in the class would not get the full account and that we would get the opportunity to trade larger only when we proved ourselves. Several in the class did receive the $1 million account Rich promised because he had faith in their ability to execute. Many others continued to trade the limited accounts we used in January for several more months.

I was surprised but pleased when Rich gave me a $2 million account to trade. Evidently he liked the way I had handled the heating oil move.

four

THINK LIKE A TURTLE

Good trading is not about being right, it is about trading right.
If you want to be successful, you need to think of the long run
and ignore the outcomes of individual trades.

After witnessing the success of the Turtles, many traders and investors have concluded that Richard Dennis won his bet with Bill Eckhardt that trading can be taught. I don't agree. I think the bet was a draw.

What people do not know is that many Turtles, perhaps one-third to one-half of them, were less profitable than the highest-performing Turtles or were not successful at all. So, although most of the Turtles learned from the experiences of that first month and over the months that followed developed into winning traders, others were dropped from the program with losing records. The difference between the best- and the worst-performing Turtles came down to their individual psychological makeup. Some took more readily to the Turtle Way than did others, proving that although trading can be taught to most people, some are better suited to it than others.

An important aspect of understanding the winning trader is understanding how his or her emotions affect trading. If you were born with the right qualities, you will find it easier to learn how to trade well; if you were not, you will need to develop those qualities. That will be your primary task. What are the *right* qualities?

It's Not about Who's Right

Winning traders think in the present and avoid thinking too much about the future. Beginners want to predict the future in their trading. When they win, they think it means they were right and they feel like heroes. When they lose, they feel like scum. That is the wrong approach.

Turtles do not care about being right. They care about making money. Turtles do not pretend to be able to predict the future. They never look at markets and say: "Gold is going up." They look at the future as unknowable in specifics but foreseeable in character. In other words, it is impossible to know whether a market is going to go up or down or whether a trend will stop now or in two months. You do know that there will be trends and that the character of price movement will not change because human emotion and cognition will not change.

It turns out that it is much easier to make money when you are wrong most of the time. If your trades are losers most of the time, that shows that you are not trying to predict the future. For this reason, you no longer care about the outcome of any particular trade since you expect that trade to lose money. When you expect a trade to lose money, you also realize that the outcome of a particular trade does not indicate anything about your intelligence. Simply put, to win you need to free yourself and your thinking of outcome bias. It does not matter what happens with any particular trade. If you have 10 losing trades in a row *and* you are sticking to your plan, you are trading well; you are just having a bit of bad luck.

Forget the Past

Ironically, as well as thinking too much about the future, most traders dwell too much on the past. They worry about what they have done, the mistakes they have made, the trades in which they have lost money.

Turtles learn from the past but don't worry about it. They don't berate themselves for mistakes they have made. They also don't criticize themselves for trades in which they lost money; they know that is part of the game.

Turtles view the past holistically and don't put any particular emphasis on recent events. The recent past is no more important than any other historical time period; it only feels that way. Turtles avoid recency bias. They know that most of the traders in the market exhibit this tendency, and for that reason, the market often shows evidence of the same bias. The ability to avoid recency bias is an important component of successful trading.

I saw the crippling effect of recency bias firsthand long after the Turtle program had ended. Once the program had been completed, each Turtle had to wait six years before the confidentiality agreements expired and we could tell others about the methods we used to trade. I had a couple of close friends who were interested in learning those methods because they knew how well the system worked for me.

In 1998 I taught one of them my methods after warning him that consistency was the key. I told him that he had to execute all the trades religiously or he would not be successful. So what did he do? He became a victim of recency bias.

Around February 1999 I asked him how he was doing in cocoa since I had noticed that there was a great downward trend. He told me that he did not take the trade because he had lost so much trading cocoa and thought that the trade was too risky. Table 4-1 shows the cocoa trades one would have encountered by trading breakouts from April 1998 until the trade with the large trend occurred. Note that there are 17 losing trades in a row in the cocoa market before a very sizable winning trade that started in November 1998.

This is typical of what you should expect to encounter in trading. If you consider a single market at a particular point in time, things can look very bleak. You may go several years before finding a single good trend in some markets. If you focus too much on the recent past, you will be tempted to think that certain markets are not tradable.

My friend was not unique. Most traders are plagued by the recent past. Some of the Turtles were affected by it so strongly during the program that they never traded successfully and finally were cut. Ironically, it seems that just about the time everyone else gives up, trends appear and tend to be easy to ride and extremely profitable. We'll examine this phenomenon in more detail later in Chapter 13 in our discussion of portfolio and market analysis.

Avoid the Future Tense

Earlier in the book we established how cognitive biases can torture potentially good traders. Recency bias, the strong need to feel that one is right, and the propensity to predict the future are to be avoided at all costs.

Table 4-1 1998 Cocoa Breakout Trades

Number	Unit	Entry	Position	Price	Quantity	Exit	%	Profit	Total
1	1	27 Apr	L	2,249	6	2,234	(2.4)	$ (1,197)	
2	1	6 May	L	2,261	6	2,246	(2.1)	$ (1,026)	
3	1	12 May	L	2,276	6	2,261	(2.2)	$ (1,036)	
4	1	14 May	L	2,283	6	2,268	(2.4)	$ (1,133)	
5	1	23 Jun	S	2,100	6	2,114	(2.3)	$ (1,061)	
6	1	25 Jun	S	2,094	6	2,108	(2.4)	$ (1,053)	
7	1	29 Jun	S	2,085	6	2,099	(3.0)	$ (1,317)	
8	1	15 Jul	S	2,070	6	2,084	(2.5)	$ (1,066)	
9	1	27 Jul	S	2,069	5	2,083	(1.9)	$ (777)	
10	1	3 Aug	S	2,050	5	2,064	(2.7)	$ (1,104)	
11	1	13 Aug	S	2,036	6	2,049	(2.2)	$ (848)	
12	1	17 Aug	S	2,024	6	2,036	(3.0)	$ (1,155)	
13	1	24 Aug	S	2,024	6	2,035	(2.4)	$ (874)	
14	1	16-Sep	S	2,014	5	2,026	(2.1)	$ (756)	
15	1	1 Oct	S	1,979	5	1,992	(2.4)	$ (845)	
16	1	13 Oct	S	1,976	5	1,988	(2.2)	$ (779)	
17	1	28 Oct	S	1,967	5	1,979	(2.1)	$ (722)	$(16,750)
18	**1**	**6 Nov**	**S**	**1,961**	**5**	**1,438**	**75.0**	**$ 24,940**	
19	2	20 Nov	S	1,918	6	1,928	(2.4)	$ (799)	
20	2	24 Nov	S	1,903	6	1,914	(3.0)	$ (975)	
21	2	30 Nov	S	1,892	5	1,903	(2.7)	$ (834)	
22	**2**	**8 Dec**	**S**	**1,873**	**5**	**1,438**	**67.2**	**$ 20,575**	
23	3	21 Dec	S	1,824	5	1,836	(3.5)	$ (1,075)	
24	3	4 Jan	S	1,808	5	1,820	(2.4)	$ (709)	
25	**3**	**15 Jan**	**S**	**1,798**	**4**	**1,438**	**46.7**	**$ 13,468**	
26	4	25 Jan	S	1,748	4	1,760	(2.1)	$ (608)	
27	4	27 Jan	S	1,742	4	1,754	(2.1)	$ (605)	
28	**4**	**8 Feb**	**S**	**1,738**	**7**	**1,438**	**42.8**	**$ 19,275**	**$55,903**

To overcome the third affliction, you need to think about the future in terms of possibilities and probabilities rather than in terms of prediction. When my circle of friends learned of my success as a Turtle, they kept asking what direction I thought a particular market would take. Everyone assumed that because I was part of a renowned trading group and had made millions trading futures, it must have been because I knew something definitive about the future. My standard response surely surprised them: "I have no idea." The truth was that I really didn't. Sure, I could have guessed, but I had absolutely no faith in my ability to predict markets. In fact, I purposely did not attempt to predict the future direction of markets.

Unfortunately, unless you happen to be an actuary working for an insurance company, you generally do not think in terms of probabilities. People tend to think in terms of likely or unlikely but never in terms of probabilities. That is why insurance companies insure against uncertain risks. An event such as a hurricane destroying your house is one such risk. There is a certain probability that there will be a hurricane that affects your house if you live near the tropical ocean. There is a slightly lower probability that the hurricane will be strong enough to damage your home. There is an even lower probability that it will be powerful enough to destroy your home completely.

If you *knew* that your house would be destroyed by a hurricane with 100 percent certainty, you would not buy insurance; you would move. Fortunately, the risk of that happening is less than 100 percent, so much less in fact that you decide to stay and insure your house.

An insurance company that insures against hurricanes will have a fairly good idea of the level of damage that is likely to occur at your particular location when it prices a policy covering such an event. This is how insurance companies make money: They sell policies to cover risks for less than the probable cost of payout under those policies.

Trading is much the same as insuring against uncertain risks. Trading is filled with uncertainties. You do not know whether a trade is going to make money. The best you can do is be confident that the rewards will outweigh the risks over the long run.

Thinking in Probabilities

Many of you took probability and statistics courses in high school or college. No doubt you would have seen a graph like the one shown in Figure 4-1.

Figure 4-1 shows what is known as a *normal distribution*. This particular graph depicts the distribution of women's height. The

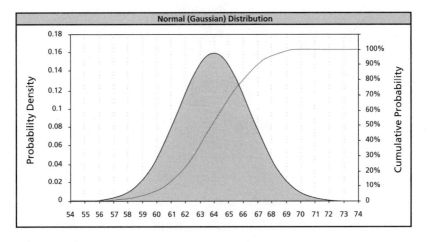

Figure 4-1   A Normal Distribution of Women's Height

bottom axis shows the height in inches, and the side axis indicates the two aspects of probability:

1. **Probability density graph:** The shaded area uses the legend on the left and shows how likely a particular height may be. In this case, the average height is 5 feet 4 inches. The probability of a woman's height being closer to that average is greater than its probability of being farther away. The higher spots in the middle of the graph indicate the most likely possibilities, and the lower height areas toward the sides indicate less likely possibilities. For example, the height of the curve at 70 inches is much lower than it is at 68 inches, indicating the lower probability that a woman will attain a height of 5 foot 10 inches compared with a height of 5 foot 8 inches.

2. **Cumulative probability curve:** The solid line runs from 0 percent to 100 percent and uses the legend on the right. It shows the cumulative probability of a woman attaining at least a particular height. For example, if you look at the green line, you can see that it reaches almost 100 percent at about the 70-inch level. The actual value at 70 inches is 99.18 percent, meaning that less than 1 percent of women are 5 foot 10 inches or taller.

This graph and others like it use complex mathematical formulas, but they all represent a simple concept: There is a decreasing likelihood of a woman attaining a particular height the farther away that height is from the center that represents the average.

But why make it so complicated to forecast probability? One could ignore the math and formulas and still construct a graph like the one shown in Figure 4-1 by using this simple method: First, go to a place where you will find a lot of women, such as a college campus. Next, find 100 women at random and measure their height. Finally, divide those heights into 1-inch intervals and count the number of women in each interval. You are fairly likely to get around 16 women at 64 inches, about 15 at 63 and 65 inches, about 12 at 62 and 66 inches, 8 at 61 and 67 inches, 4 at 60 and 68 inches, 2 at 59 and 69 inches, and one each at 58 and 70 inches.

If you created a bar chart showing the number of women at each particular height, it would look like the chart shown in Figure 4-2.

The type of graph shown in Figure 4-2 is called a *histogram*. It graphically shows the frequency of a particular measure compared with other nearby measures (in this case the measure of a woman's height). The graph in Figure 4-2 has the same shape as

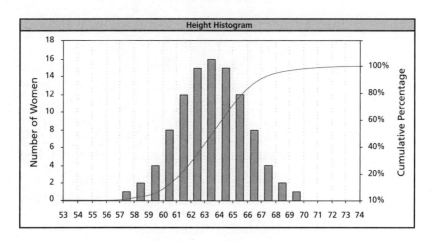

Figure 4-2   A Histogram of Women's Heights

the normal distribution graph in Figure 4-1, but it also has the advantage of being something you can construct without using complex mathematical formulas. You only need to be able to count and categorize.

A histogram like this can be constructed from your trading systems to give you an idea of how the future might turn out; it provides you with a way to think in terms of probabilities rather than prediction. Figure 4-3 is a histogram of monthly returns from a 20-year test of a simplified version of the Turtle system, the Donchian Trend system. In addition to being simpler, it has a better performance record than the Turtle system.

The histogram sections in Figure 4-3 are divided into 2 percent segments. One bar lists the number of months with between 0 percent and 2 percent positive returns, the next bar lists the number between 2 percent and 4 percent, and so on. Note how the shape of the histogram resembles the normal distribution of heights described above. The notable difference is that the shape is elongated toward the right. This elongation represents the good months and sometimes is referred to as *skew* and *fat tails*.

The histogram shown in Figure 4-4 represents the distribution of the trades themselves. Figure 4-4 shows how individual trades are distributed. The section on the left is for losing trades, and the section on the right is for winning trades. Note that the scales for each section include both a number scale on the outside left and right and a percentage scale in the middle from 0 percent to 100 percent. The cumulative lines move from 0 percent to 100 percent from the center of the graph outward.

The numeric legends on the left and right indicate the number of trades represented by each 20 percent section of the graph. For

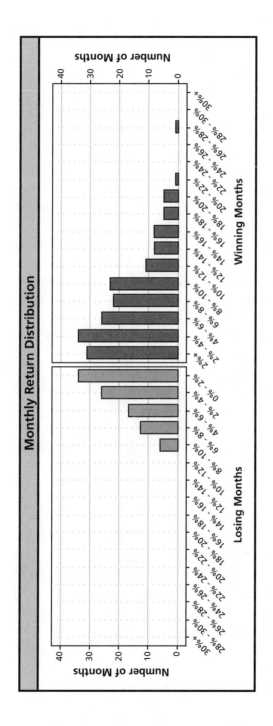

Figure 4-3 Distribution of Monthly Returns

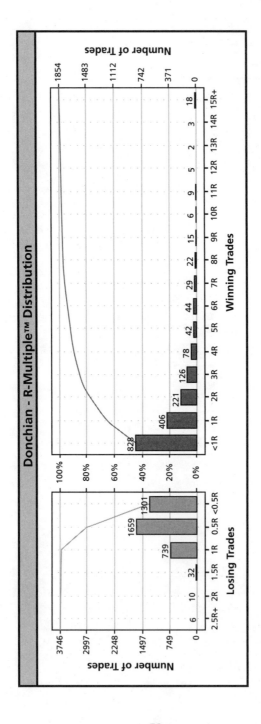

Figure 4-4 Distribution of Trade Outcomes

example, the 100 percent level for losing trades is 3,746, which means that there were 3,746 losing trades during the 22 years of the test. The corresponding 100 percent level for winning trades is 1,854 trades.

The trades are divided into bars on the basis of the amount of profit they earned divided by the amount risked on a trade. This concept is known as an *R-multiple* and was invented by the trader Chuck Branscomb as a convenient way to compare trades between systems and between markets. (R-multiples were popularized by Van Tharp in his book *Trade Your Way to Financial Freedom*.)

An example will help illustrate this system. If you buy a contract of August gold at $450 with a stop at $440 in case the trade goes against you, you have $1,000 at risk since the $10 difference between $450 and $440 multiplied by the 100 ounces in a contract totals $1,000. If that trade earns $5,000 in profit, it is called a 5R trade because the $5,000 profit is five times the amount of the money that was risked ($1,000). In Figure 4-4, the winning trades are divided into buckets at 1R intervals and losing trades are divided into buckets at ½R intervals.

It may seem odd that in this histogram the losing trades outnumber the winning trades by so much. This is actually a very common occurrence in trend-following systems. However, although the number of losing trades is very high, the system keeps most losses close to the desired entry risk of 1R. Winning trades, in contrast, are many times the entry risk, with 43 trades returning 10 or more times the entry risk.

How does this help one think like a Turtle?

As Turtles, we never knew which trade would end up being a winner and which a loser. We just knew the general shape of the distribution of possible outcomes we might encounter: A distribution much like the ones shown in the graphs above. We thought that each trade *possibly* could be a winner but that most *probably* would be losers. And we knew that some would be medium-sized winners of 4 to 5R and some would be large winners of 12R or even 20R or 30R. But ultimately, the Turtles knew that the winners would be large enough to cover the losses from the losing trades and that there would be profit left over.

Thus, when we made a trade, we did not measure our personal worth by the outcome of the trade because we knew it most likely would be a losing trade. We thought in terms of probabilities, and that gave us the confidence to make decisions in the face of large degrees of risk and uncertainty.

Dos and Don'ts for Thinking Like a Turtle

1. **Trade in the present:** Do not dwell on the past or try to predict the future. The former is counterproductive, and the latter is impossible.

2. **Think in terms of probabilities, not prediction:** Instead of trying to be right by predicting the market, focus on methods in which the probabilities are in your favor for a successful outcome over the long run.

3. **Take responsibility for your own trades:** Don't blame your mistakes and failures on others, the markets, your broker, and so forth. Take responsibility for your mistakes and learn from them.

Playing Favorites

Some of the Turtles had a hard time with this concept; they felt the need to be right and to predict the markets. For this reason, even after the first month's heating oil example, they did not trade consistently. I remember one in particular who was convinced that Rich had given me and a few of the others secret rules that he had not shared with the class at large. That idea was completely ludicrous. Why would Rich intentionally leave out important information and then give traders his own money for them to lose, not to mention losing his bet?

There were no hidden secrets. The truth was that I actually used a much simpler trading method than most of the other Turtles employed. I traded using 100 percent of my account allocated to the longer-term 10-week breakout system. This meant fewer trades and less monitoring of the markets. I certainly was not doing anything unusual or acting on information that had not been made public.

Excuses, Excuses

The idea that Rich had left out some key ideas was the easiest way for our paranoid Turtle to explain his inability to trade successfully during the program. This is a common problem in trading and in life. Many people blame their failure on others or on circumstances outside their control. They fail and then blame everyone but themselves. Inability to take responsibility for one's own actions and their consequences is probably the single most significant factor leading to failure.

Trading is a good way to break that habit. In the end, it is only you and the markets. You cannot hide from the markets. If you trade well, over the long run you will see good results. If you trade poorly, over the long run you will lose money. Despite the obvious and unavoidable link between what you do and your trading results, some people still try to blame the markets. They invent scenarios in which the "specialists" or another mysterious group of traders conspires to steal their money rather than taking the blame for their own trading mistakes.

Although there is no question that there many traders endeavoring to take your money at any point in time, I have never seen any evidence of mass-scale collusion or fraud of the kind imagined by those who blame their failures on the market, their brokers, or other participants.

The bottom line is that *you make the trades and you are responsible for the outcome*. Don't blame anyone else for giving you bad advice or withholding secrets from you. If you screw up and do something stupid, learn from that mistake, don't pretend you didn't make it. Then go figure out a way to avoid making that same mistake in the future.

Blaming others for your mistakes is a sure way to lose.

TRADING WITH AN EDGE

Trading with an edge is what separates the professionals from the amateurs. Ignore this and you will be eaten by those who don't.

Trading is about buying at one price and then selling at a higher price later or selling short at a particular price and then buying to exit the short position at a later point. When they are determining when to enter a market, most beginners employ a strategy that is no better than throwing darts at the chart. Experienced traders would say that their strategy has no edge. The term *edge* is borrowed from gambling theory and refers to the statistical advantage held by the casino. It also refers to the advantage that can be gained by counting cards when one is playing blackjack. Without an edge in games of chance, you will lose money in the long run.

This is true in trading as well. If you do not have an edge, the costs of trading will cause you to lose money. Commissions, slippage, computer costs, and exchange and pricing data fees add up very quickly. *An edge in trading is an exploitable statistical advantage based on market behavior that is likely to recur in the future.* In trading, the best edges come from the market behaviors caused by cognitive biases.

Elements of an Edge

To find an edge, you need to locate entry points where there is a greater than normal probability that the market will move in a particular direction within your desired time frame. You then pair those entries with an exit strategy designed to profit from the type of moves for which the entry is designed. Simply put, to maximize your edge, entry strategies should be paired with exit strategies. Thus, trend-following entry strategies can be paired with many different types of trend-following exit strategies, countertrend entry strategies can be paired with many different countertrend exit strategies, swing trading entries can be paired with many different types of swing trading exit strategies, and so on.

To understand why this is important, let's dig further into the components that make up the edge for a system. System edges come from three components:

- **Portfolio selection:** The algorithms that select which markets are valid for trading on any specific day
- **Entry signals:** The algorithms that determine when to buy or sell to enter a trade
- **Exit signals:** The algorithms that determine when to buy or sell to exit a trade

It is possible for an entry signal to have an edge that is significant for the short term but not for the medium term or long term. Conversely, it is possible to have an exit signal that has an edge for long-term systems but not for the short term. Some concrete examples will help demonstrate this effect.

The Edge Ratio (E-Ratio)

When you are examining entry signals, you care about the price movement subsequent to the occurrence of the market actions that constitute the signal. One way to look at this movement is to break the price movement into two parts: the good part and the bad part.

Good price movement is that which progresses in the direction of the trade. In other words, when you buy, it's good when a market moves up and bad when it moves down, and when you sell short, it's good when a market moves down and bad when it moves up. Consider the case where a buy results in a price that initially moves in a direction that is bad for the trade, the price goes down; then it goes up and moves to a price higher than the entry price for the trade; after this move down, the price moves up for a while and then goes down again, as shown in Figure 5.1.

Traders refer to the maximum move in the bad direction as the *maximum adverse excursion* (MAE) and the maximum move in the good direction as the *maximum favorable excursion* (MFE). Thus, the lines with the double arrows in the figure show the size of the MAE and MFE for the price move indicated. Figure 5-1 demonstrates the case where the MFE (good price movement) is much higher than the MAE (bad price movement).

You can use these to measure the edge of an entry signal directly. If a certain entry signal generates a move in which the average maximum good movement was higher than the average maximum bad

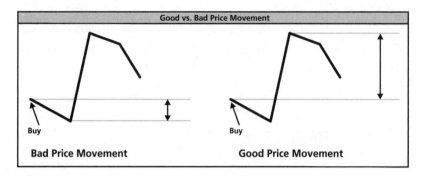

Figure 5-1 Good versus Bad Price Movement

movement (i.e., the average MFE was higher than the average MAE), this would indicate that a positive edge existed. If the average MAE (adverse movement) was higher than the average MFE (good movement), this would indicate that a negative edge existed. One would expect that a truly random entry would result in approximately the same good movement as bad movement. For example, take the case in which one bought if a coin landed heads up and sold if it landed tails up. One would expect that the price movement subsequent to this type of entry would have an MFE equal to its MAE.

To turn this way of thinking about an edge of an entry into a concrete way of measuring the edge for entry signals, it is necessary to add a few more steps. First, you need a way to equate price movement across different markets. Second, you need a way to determine the time period over which to measure the average MFE and average MAE. To normalize the MFE and MAE across markets so that you can compare the averages meaningfully, you can use the same mechanism the Turtles used to normalize the size of our trades across markets: equating them by using the *average true range* (ATR).

To isolate the behavior of entries over various markets, it is useful to be able to compare the price behavior of an entry signal across different time frames. I usually examine a specific number of days and then measure the MFE and MAE for that number of days after each signal is generated. At Trading Blox, where I head Research and Development for a sophisticated system-testing environment, we have implemented an entry edge measure we call the *E-ratio* (short for edge ratio).

The E-ratio combines all of the pieces described above by using the following formula:

1. Compute the MFE and MAE for the time frame specified.

2. Divide each of them by the ATR at entry to adjust for volatility and normalize across markets.

3. Sum each of these values separately and divide by the total number of signals to get the average volatility-adjusted MFE and MAE.

4. The E-ratio is the average volatility-adjusted MFE divided by the average volatility-adjusted MAE.

To define the time frame, we use the number of days in the description of the ratio to indicate the number of days over which the component MFE and MAE were computed. For example, an E10-ratio measurement computes the MFE and MAE for 10 days, including the day of entry; an E50-ratio uses 50 days, and so on.

The E-ratio can be used to measure whether an entry has an edge. For example, you can use it to test whether a completely random entry has any edge. To illustrate, I ran a test of the E-ratio for the period of the last 10 years by using an entry that randomly enters long or short at the open, depending on the computer equivalent of a coin flip. The average of 30 individual tests showed an E5-ratio of 1.01, an E10-ratio of 1.005, and an E50-ratio of 0.997. These numbers are very close to the 1.0 we would expect, and if we ran more trials, the numbers would get closer and closer to 1.0. This is the case because the price is just as likely to go against a position as it is to go in a direction favorable to a position over any reasonable time period.

You can also use the E-ratio to examine the major components of the Donchian Trend system. The two major components of the entries for this system are a Donchian channel breakout and a trend portfolio filter. The Donchian channel breakout is a rule that states that one should buy when the price exceeds the highest high of the previous 20 days and sell short when the price goes lower than the lowest low of the previous 20 days. The trend portfolio filter means that you can initiate long trades only in markets in which the 50-day moving average is *higher* than the 300-day moving average and can initiate short trades only in markets in which the 50-day moving average is *lower* than the 300-day moving average. One of the roles of the portfolio filter is to eliminate markets that are not in a market state favorable to this system.

Let me show you how to use the E-ratio to examine the trade-entry rules for the Donchian Trend system. All the tests described below were performed by using a set of 28 high-volume U.S. futures markets, employing data from January 1, 1996, to June 30, 2006.

The E5-ratio for our sample is 0.99, and the E10-ratio is 1.0. "Wait a minute," you might say. "I thought that the E-ratio would be greater than 1 when an entry had a positive edge." This is true. However, remember that we need to consider that the Donchian channel breakout system is a medium-term, trend-following system, so its entry needs to have an edge over the medium term, not the short term. One might say more generally that an entry needs to have an edge only over the time frame for the system in which it is being used.

The E70-ratio for our entry is 1.20, which means that trades taken in the direction of a 20-day breakout move on average 20 percent farther in the direction of the breakout than they do in the opposite direction when one looks at the price movement in the 70 days subsequent to the entry signal.

Figure 5-2 shows how the edge ratio changes for 20-day breakouts over varying numbers of days. First, the edge ratio starts off below 1.0, meaning that over the very short term there is generally more movement against a trade taken at a breakout than there is in the direction of the breakout. This is one of the reasons trading breakouts can be very difficult psychologically. It is also one of the reasons you can make money using a countertrend trading style by betting on the breakout not holding and in favor of a bounce off of the support or resistance. There is a positive edge for these strategies in the very short term.

Second, the edge ratio begins to climb steadily but still fluctuates fairly erratically on the positive side of 1.0, indicating a positive edge but one where it is difficult to quantify with true precision.

The Trend Portfolio Filter Edge

How do the portfolio selection criteria affect the edge for the Donchian channel system? You can examine this in two ways. First, you can look at how the portfolio selection filter affects the edge of purely random entries and compare them with the baseline edge

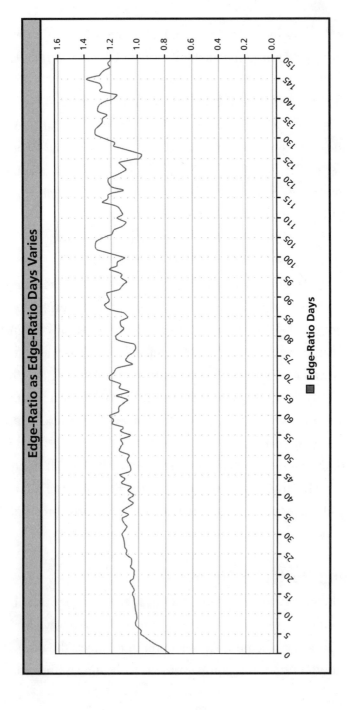

Figure 5-2 Edge Ratio as Number of Days Varies

ratio of 1.0 for random entries without any portfolio filtering. Second, you can combine the filter with our entry signals to see how the portfolio trend filter affects the edge ratio of our breakout signals.

Running a test of 70,000 random entries with the trend portfolio filter shows a remarkable E70-ratio of 1.27. This is even greater than the E70-ratio for the entry signal itself. This serves as a clear indication that this portfolio selection algorithm increases the edge of the system.

Using a trend portfolio filter substantially increases the likelihood of movement in the direction of a trade taken with a breakout. The E70-ratio for our example moved from 1.20 to 1.33. Further, the use of a trend filter combined with a breakout changes the shape and smoothness of the resulting edge ratio graph (Figure 5-3).

Notice how much smoother the graph in Figure 5-3 is and how much higher the edge ratio climbs after we add the trend portfolio filter. The graph shows that the E120-ratio is about 1.6.

The reason for this result is that breakout trades that go against the long-term trend have been eliminated. Those trades were a source of many of the significant moves against the initial position since breakouts that occur in the direction opposite a trend are much less likely to result in significant continuation. These breakouts are also indicative of the market being in a state which is not as favorable to the Donchian Trend system.

The Exit Edge

Even the exit signals for a system should have an edge if possible. Unfortunately, it is somewhat more difficult to measure the edge of an exit. This is the case because exits are dependent on the condi-

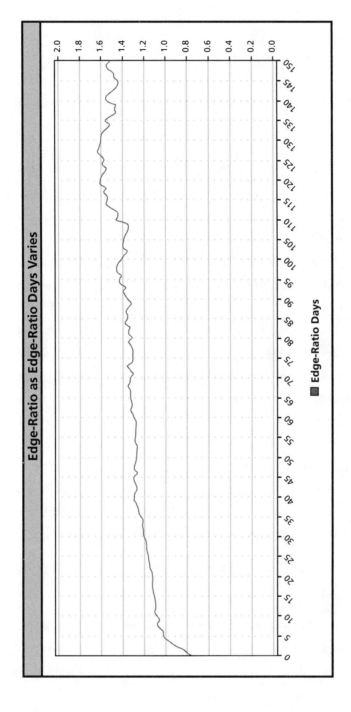

Figure 5-3   Edge Ratio with Addition of Trend Filter

tions of both the entry and the exit signals. In other words, you cannot isolate an exit from the conditions that cause a position to be initiated. There is a more complex set of interactions between the various elements of a system rather than just a single component.

Since it is a more complex system, you are less concerned with the edge of an exit than with its effect on the measurement criteria of the system itself. For this reason, it is better to measure the effect of an exit on those measurements which matter most rather than simply by looking at what happens after the exit. Furthermore, when you are looking at entries into the market, you are indeed concerned with what happens after you enter, since that is the period in which your money is in play. Traders make money only when they are in the market.

Exits are different. What happens after an exit does not affect your results; only what happens before the exit has an effect. For these reasons, you should judge exits on the basis of how they affect the performance of the entire system.

FALLING OFF
THE EDGE

*Edges are found in the places that are the battlegrounds
between buyers and sellers. Your task as a trader is to find
those places and wait to see who wins and who loses.*

Trading edges exist because of divergences in market perceptions and realities that result from cognitive biases. They exist
because economists are wrong in their belief that market players
are rational. Market players are not rational. Chapter 2 discussed
how cognitive biases provide trading opportunities in a theoretical
sense. This chapter will discuss that notion in further detail by
using actual price data.

Support and Resistance

The concept of *support and resistance* is fundamental to almost all
types of trading. Support and resistance is simply the tendency for
prices not to exceed previous price levels. One can understand this
concept most easily by examining its presence on a price chart (see
Figure 6-1).

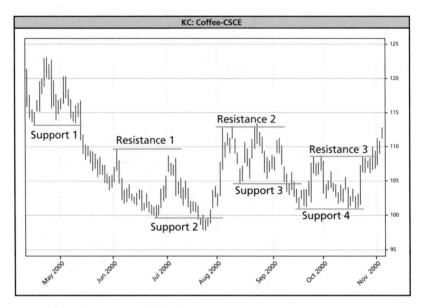

Figure 6-1 Support and Resistance Levels
Copyright 2006 Trading Blox, LLC. All rights reserved worldwide.

Support and resistance results from market behavior, which in turn is caused by three cognitive biases: anchoring, recency bias, and the disposition effect.

Anchoring is the tendency to base price perceptions on readily available information. A recent new high or low becomes a new anchor against which each subsequent price is measured and compared. New prices are considered to be higher or lower in comparison to those anchor prices. The reason recent highs and lows are easy anchors is that they are simple to see on the charts and therefore are psychologically significant to market participants.

In Figure 6-1, under the label "Support 1," a low price of about $1.13 becomes a new anchor shortly after that price is made and certainly after the price climbs to $1.20 over the next several days. It is the low point on the chart that will stand out for short-term day traders and longer-term position traders alike. As the price descends back to the range of $1.15, over the days after the high at about $1.23, traders continue to think in terms of the previous but still recent $1.13 low. At $1.15 they will judge the price as low but not *too* low on the basis of a comparison with that anchor price at $1.13.

Recency bias is the tendency for people to place greater importance on more recent data and experience. Since the low at $1.13 was recent, it will count more in a trader's evaluation of the current price than will other previous lows. That low will have a greater meaning to the market participant because of this bias. How does this affect the support and resistance phenomenon?

Imagine that you are a trader who wants to buy coffee. When the price first went to $1.13, you might have wished or hoped that it would go even lower and therefore might not have purchased coffee at that price. As the price climbed to $1.23 over the next several days, you would have been very unhappy that you did not buy any coffee below $1.15 because you are now anchoring on that recent $1.13 low which becomes the basis for a more concrete sense of a "low" price. Thus, when the price drops below $1.15 a few days later, you will be much more likely to buy even though the price is the same as it was the last time the price was there a few days earlier. The effect of anchoring and the recency bias will cause you to consider any price below $1.15 as reasonably low and therefore a good price at which to buy. Since many market participants similarly consider a price below $1.15 as good, any pause in the price movement below that price probably will result in more buyers coming into the market. This influx of new buyers at points of support creates a tendency for market prices to bounce off the price levels of previous highs and lows.

The perception of most traders that support and resistance is a real phenomenon adds to the reality of its existence because the market behavior of those who believe in it by itself reinforces that phenomenon. If many traders believe that there will be significant buying when a price drops to a certain level, they will be more inclined to believe that the price will rise once it reaches that level. This belief in and of itself will reduce their willingness to sell at or near that price since they will prefer to sell later, after the price has risen—because of the effect of support at the price. The belief in support and resistance causes it to become a self-fulfilling prophecy.

The disposition effect is the tendency for traders to want to lock in profits rather than let winning trades get larger. Traders' fear of losing profits grows stronger as those profits rise. How does this affect support and resistance?

Imagine that you were a trader who bought coffee in early August at 102 just after the end of the area labeled "Support 2" in Figure 6-1. When the price rose to 114 over the next several days, you probably would not have sold because the price moved so quickly in your favor that you would have believed that it might go as high as 120 or 125. Subsequently, when the price dropped to 105, you found yourself wishing that you had sold it over 110. The recent high would have had you thinking, "If the price gets over 114 again, I am going to sell this time."

Thus, when the price does in fact go back up to that level, you want to lock in your profits and sell at that time. There probably will be many others in a similar position who also will want to sell when the price again approaches those recent highs (the area labeled "Resistance 2"). This creates a natural barrier at that price because many traders will want to sell at what they consider a *high* price. Since the previous highs set in early August become the *anchor* against which subsequent prices are measured, prices that approach that price are considered high. Therefore, more and more traders are willing to sell as the price approaches those highs.

Finding the Edge in Support and Resistance

Like many aspects of trading, the concept of support and resistance is a loose construct rather than a hard-and-fast rule. Prices are not guaranteed to bounce off former highs and lows; they just tend to. Prices are not guaranteed to bounce off the exact price of a high and a low; sometimes they react a bit before, sometimes a bit after, and sometimes not at all.

If one is employing a countertrend strategy, support and resistance is the direct source of the edge. The tendency for prices to bounce off previous highs and lows is what provides the edge for countertrend traders. When support and resistance holds up, the countertrend traders who rely on its effect will make money.

If one is using a trend-following system, the breakdown of support and resistance is what matters. Consider what happened when the support level did not hold in the case of the December 2006 heating oil contract (see Figure 6-2).

The support at $2.10 per gallon held the first time it was tested in mid-June. The price bounced off $2.10 and then stopped at $2.31, which served as a new resistance level. When the price bounced off the support line at $2.16, it went higher but was unable to exceed the resistance level at $2.31. Note what happened the second time the price reached the level marked "Support 2." This time the price hesitated, showing that there was some buying pressure at

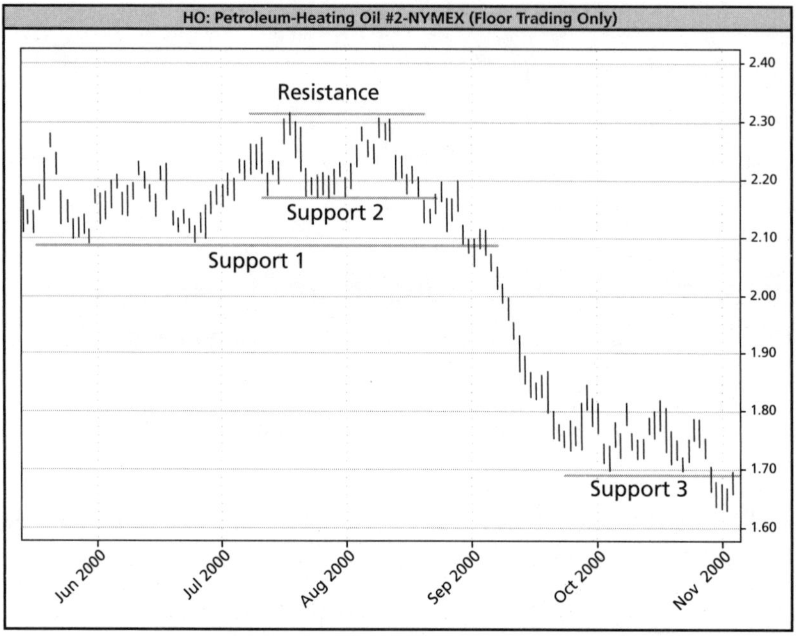

Figure 6-2 Support Breaks Down
Copyright 2006 Trading Blox, LLC. All rights reserved worldwide.

that price but it did not hold up. The price dropped below the "Support 1" line, where it initially also moved upward for a few days, showing that there was some buying pressure at that level as well.

It is what happened next that is the most interesting, especially if you consider the likely psychological perspectives of the various market participants. On September 5, the price dropped and closed below the previous low at $2.05, which had been set on August 30, just three trading days earlier. That meant that anyone who recently had initiated a long position by buying heating oil in anticipation of higher prices was holding a losing trade. Further, there were no recent price points that one could expect would offer support, meaning that there was a significant possibility that if the price fell, it might fall quite a bit. As Figure 6-2 indicates, this is exactly what happened. The price fell all the way to $1.85, where there was some weak buying, probably as a result of a previous support line at that level seven months earlier. This line did not hold, and the price did not start to come back up until late September after hitting a low of $1.73.

Smart countertrend traders would have been out near or on the close on September 5 or perhaps the following morning. They know that sometimes support holds and sometimes it doesn't, and you do not want to fight the market when it does not or you could be wiped out. This could have been one of those instances.

Imagine that you had been bullish on heating oil and had bought 5 contracts at $2.10 in anticipation of higher prices; you might have bought 5 more contracts at $2.05 as the price became even cheaper when measured against the anchor of the recent $2.10 price support level. What would you have been thinking as the price dropped below $2.00 or $1.90 and then broke $1.80 a few days later? That small 5-contract trade that developed into a 10-contract losing trade would now be a whopping $115,500 loss (10 contracts with a $0.275 per gallon loss per contract on average with each contract being for 42,000 gallons).

This kind of thing happens all the time to new traders. They panic and find themselves on the wrong side of the market when it moves swiftly and suddenly against them. Trend followers love these occurrences because they are selling on the way down, and as the market makes new lows, they are making money.

The source of the edge for trend followers is the gap in human perception at the time when support and resistance breaks down. At those times, people hold on to previous beliefs for too long and the market does not move quickly enough to reflect the new reality.

That is why there is a statistically significant tendency for the markets to move further when support and resistance breaks down than at other times.

In the case above, there are no new buyers at the prices below the initial resistance at the end of the "Support 1" line. If you wanted to buy heating oil and the price was dropping below $2.05, why would you buy there? You wouldn't; you would wait until the price had stopped dropping. Why buy now if the price is dropping? Yet as the price continues to drop, even more people who need to sell will panic, sending the price lower and lower. This will continue until the selling exhausts itself and some of those who wish to buy start to believe that the price will not drop further.

The Turtles saw this happen time and time again. Sometimes we were initiating positions, and during those times we were happy with the subsequent price movements. Sometimes we were exiting positions, and at those times we were among those trying to exit our profitable positions as we saw the support break down.

A breakout occurs when the price "breaks out" of previous resistance and support levels. As breakout traders, we were buying resistance breakdowns to enter long trades and selling support breakdowns to enter short trades. We sold short-term support breakdowns to exit long trades and bought short-term resistance breakdowns to exit short trades.

Shaky Ground

The prices near the edges of support and resistance represent what I call *points of price instability*. They represent places where prices are unlikely to remain but are more likely to move higher or lower. In the

[handwritten margin note: OPTION : BREAKOUT TRADING]

case where support holds, the price moves higher. In the case where resistance holds, the price moves lower, bouncing off the resistance. In cases where support and resistance do not hold, the prices continue to move in the direction of the breakdown and often do so for quite some distance. When a price level has been broken that the market has not seen for some time, there is generally no obvious subsequent point where one is likely to encounter further support or resistance. There are no remaining obvious anchors that might serve as potential turning points for change in trader psychology.

In both of the examples described above, the price is not likely to remain at the unstable price point. That is why I use the word *unstable* to describe those points. There is too much pressure at those points. One side or the other will win the battle of psychological warfare, and as the exhausted side gives up, the price will move up or down. It generally will not stay where it was. Points of price instability represent good trading opportunities. This is the case because at these points there is a relatively small price difference between a trade working and not working. This means that the cost of being wrong is lower.

The battle analogy is apt for another reason. In classic battles, the General of the attacking army waits until the best opportunity for success presents itself. He may send small forays to test the defenses of the enemy, but he does not put the full weight of his army into the attack until the proper time. When prices are in between support and resistance levels, each side is not really engaged in the battle so it is difficult to see who will win or lose. As the prices draw closer to those levels each side becomes more and more committed. One of the sides will lose. The price cannot both break out *and* fail to break out. It will do one or the other.

It is easiest to tell who will win a battle when it is nearly over. It is also easiest to tell whether the buyer or seller will win the psychological battle of support and resistance after they've engaged and you can see the price either continuing to break out through that support or resistance or clearly bouncing off of it.

Using Figure 6-2 as an example, a countertrend trader who bought at $2.10 in anticipation of an upward move could place a stop 6¢ below that entry, as that price would represent a breakdown of the support. Likewise, a trend-following trader who sold the breakout at $2.10 could place a stop $0.05 or $0.06 above the entry at $2.15 or $2.16. A price that reached those levels after hitting $2.10 would be showing enough strength to indicate that the support was holding.

Edges come from places where there are systematic misperceptions as a result of cognitive biases. Those places are the battle-grounds between buyers and sellers. Good traders examine the evidence and place bets on what they perceive to be the winning side. They also learn to admit when they have made the wrong bet and quickly fix the situation by exiting the trade. Subsequent chapters will build on these concepts and look at complete systems.

BY WHAT MEASURE?

Mature understanding of and respect for risk is the
hallmark of the best traders. They know that if you don't keep
an eye on risk, it will set its eye on you.

A key question, perhaps the only question, to ask when you are considering a system-based trading strategy or trying to select a fund advisor who uses such a strategy is: "How can you know whether a system or a manager is a good one?" In general, the answers the industry offers are various takes on the following: The strategy or manager with the highest risk/reward ratio.

Everyone wants to make the most money for a specific level of risk or incur the least risk for a particular level of expected return. On this point we are almost all in agreement: traders, investors, fund operators, and so forth. Unfortunately, there are many different opinions on the best measures of the risk and reward parts of the risk/reward ratio. Sometimes the financial industry defines risk in such a way that the description completely blinds it to certain kinds of risks, and those risks are just as likely to bite them in the ass as are the ones with which they do concern themselves.

The large losses incurred in the implosion of Long-Term Capital Management are a good example of risks that existed outside the traditional measures. This chapter will review those risks and ways to account for them, and then propose some general mechanisms for estimating risk and reward for trading systems by using historical data.

Rich and Bill were very concerned with the size of our positions because they knew that there was a risk of losing their entire net worth if those positions were too large during a large adverse price movement. A few years before starting the Turtle program, they had traded during a period when the silver market was locked down limit for days and days. This meant that there was no opportunity to exit because there were no traders willing to buy within the limits imposed by the COMEX futures exchange on how much the price of silver could change in a single day. This is the futures trader's worst nightmare. Each day you are losing more and more money and there is nothing you can do about it.

Fortunately, Rich was able to trim his position before this occurred, and that probably saved him tens of millions of dollars. If he had not acted quickly, he would have lost everything. I am sure the memory of that move was vivid in their minds during the Turtle program.

Rich constantly monitored the Turtles' positions and sometimes would reduce his own positions if he felt that the aggregate risk was too great. Contrary to the popular notion that Rich was sometimes a gunslinger, in my experience he was very careful with his risk.

Risky Business

Because there are many different types of risk, there are many different ways of measuring it. There are big risks that may come from relatively infrequent occurrences, those which happen once or twice a decade; there are more common risks that one might expect to occur a few times each year. Most traders worry about four primary risks:

- **Drawdowns:** Strings of losses that reduce the capital in their trading accounts

- **Low returns:** Periods of small gains in which one does not make enough money to live on

- **Price shocks:** Sudden movements in one or more markets that result in a large unrecoverable loss

- **System death:** A change in market dynamics that causes a previously profitable system to start losing money

Let's examine each of these risks and then consider assessments that can be incorporated into risk/reward measures for evaluating traders and trading systems.

Drawdowns

The drawdown is probably the risk that causes the most traders to stop trading and results in the most traders ending up as net losers. The equity curve shown in Figure 7-1 represents the results of trading with an account of $100,000 from January 1996 until May 2006 using the Donchian Trend system.

From the graph, you can see that the equity has grown at an average compounded rate of 43.7 percent over the slightly more than 10 years of the test. There was also a period during the test that exhibited a 38 percent drawdown.

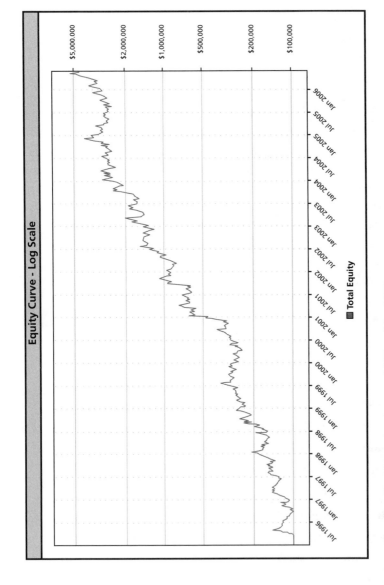

Figure 7-1 Donchian Trend Results: January 1996 to May 2006

Many new traders will be seduced by the profits of a system with results like this, thinking, "Surely I can sustain a 38 percent loss in return for these kinds of profits." Unfortunately, experience has shown time and again that people are not very good at estimating their tolerance for these sorts of things. This is especially the case if all you are looking at is a graph like the one in Figure 7-1, which uses a logarithmic scale that tends to make drawdowns look smaller than they look on a standard scale.

Confident in the results of this system and in his ability to withstand these sorts of drawdowns, trader John Newbie begins trading on June 1 with $100,000. Figure 7-2 shows the same results as those in Figure 7-1 updated until the end of October 2006, using a linear scale that outlines the historical drawdowns.

Shortly after Newbie begins trading on June 1, the system enters a period of drawdown that is slightly higher than anything shown in previous tests: a drawdown of 42 percent. What is going through his mind at this point?

Lots of doubts, fear, anxiety, and countless questions:

"What if the system has stopped working?"

"What if this is just the beginning of an even larger drawdown?"

"What if there was something wrong with the way I did my testing?"

"What if . . .?"

These types of doubts often cause a new trader to stop using the system or start selectively taking trades to "reduce risk." Many times this results in the trader missing out on winning trades, and in a

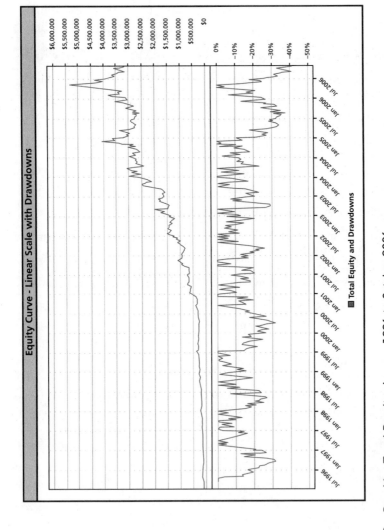

Figure 7-2 Donchian Trend Results: January 1996 to October 2006

frustrated state, after having lost one-half or more of the initial account, the trader bails. This is the major reason new traders are unsuccessful even when they use valid strategies: They have over-estimated their ability to withstand the large fluctuations that come from trading at aggressive risk levels.

From my personal observations, most people cannot sustain drawdowns of this sort. A successful trader who has a lot of confidence in his trading, his system, and his testing may be able to withstand a large drawdown, but a prudent new trader should adjust his risk accordingly to reduce the likely drawdowns. This inevitably also means reducing the returns that will come from trading the system. That is a wise compromise.

As Turtles, we were lucky since our boss, Richard Dennis, did not look at drawdowns that happened as a result of giving back profits in the same way that he looked at drawdowns that happened because of a string of losses. He knew that giving back part of the profits was a part of the game for trend followers.

For that reason, he was a very easy boss for whom to manage money. Most other investors would have panicked with the kinds of drawdowns we sometimes incurred. If you look at the returns of the former Turtles who have been the most successful at raising outside money, you will see that they are trading at a greatly reduced level from their Turtle days. This is practically a requirement if you want to raise institutional money.

Unfortunately, you cannot make the 100 percent plus returns we did as Turtles without drawdowns at these levels. I think my worst drawdown was something on the order of 70 percent. I don't know many people who can sustain that level of drawdown. It is very difficult on most people's psyches.

Low Returns

If a trader is expecting to achieve returns of 30 percent per trade, this goal can be achieved by using a system that returns 30 percent each year reliably or by one that returns 5 percent in year 1, 5 percent in year 2, and 100 percent in year 3. After three years, each of these systems will have returned the same average CAGR (compound average growth rate) of 30 percent. However, most traders would argue that a system that returned 30 percent each year would be preferable because it would offer a smoother equity curve.

All else being equal, we have found that a system that consistently delivers good returns will be more likely to offer good returns in any future period. Therefore, the risk of having that system deliver subpar returns in any given single year will be lower than for a system that had more erratic historical returns.

Price Shocks

A price shock is a sudden or very rapid movement in price that generally is caused by a natural catastrophe, unforeseen political event, or economic disaster. Since I started trading, there have been two very notable price shocks: the U.S. stock market crash of 1987 with its subsequent financial repercussions and the September 11, 2001 attack on the World Trade Center in New York City.

The first price shock occurred when I was trading a $20 million account for Richard Dennis. I remember it well. I actually made a bit of money on the day of the crash, but the next day was a different story.

Eurodollars closed on Black Monday, October 19, 1987, at 90.64, close to their contract low of 90.15 that had been set two days previously and had been tested earlier that morning with a low at 90.18. I was short something like 1,200 contracts of December eurodollars and another 600 T-bills. I also had significant long positions in gold and silver and large positions in a few currencies.

The next morning the eurodollar opened up at 92.85, more than two points higher and about $5,500 per contract without any opportunity to exit. This was a price we had not seen in eight months. Additionally, gold opened down $25 and silver opened down over $1. Figure 7-3 shows the eurodollar market on the day of this price shock.

In total, I was down about $11 million on the $20 million account I was trading for Richard Dennis. Essentially my entire year's profits had vanished *overnight*.

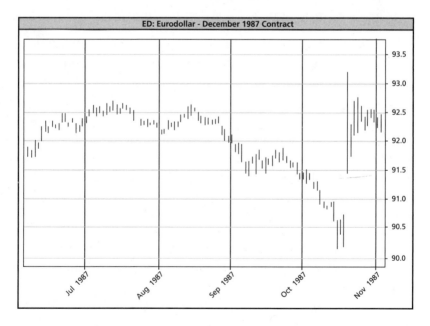

Figure 7-3   Effect of Price Shock on Eurodollar Price

It was amusing in an ironic sense that the day of the crash I made money. It was the government freaking out and lowering interest rates overnight with no warning that killed me. Now that was a price shock.

Figure 7-4 is a graph that shows an initial trading account of $100,000 using the Donchian Trend system from the time we started trading as Turtles in 1984 until the end of 1987.

You can clearly see the large spike representing a 65 percent drawdown. It is important to remember that that drawdown occurred overnight. There was no chance to exit the market. It is also interesting to note that the drawdown from that single day was twice anything the system would have indicated through historical testing. In other words, the historical testing would have understated the drawdown by a factor of 2.

All traders who wish to stay in business would be prudent to keep the reality of price shocks in mind as they settle on an appropriate risk level for their accounts. Anyone who wants to earn high returns runs an equally high risk of experiencing a high drawdown or even a total loss of her entire trading equity if a large price shock occurs.

System Death

System death is the risk that a system that has been working or that appears to have worked on the basis of historical testing suddenly stops functioning and starts losing money. This risk comes more from relying on poor testing methods than from the markets themselves. It is also a larger risk for those who trade short-term systems that have been optimized for recent price action.

For a new trader it may be quite difficult to distinguish between a system that is merely in a drawdown period and one that genuinely has stopped working. I would venture that this is probably

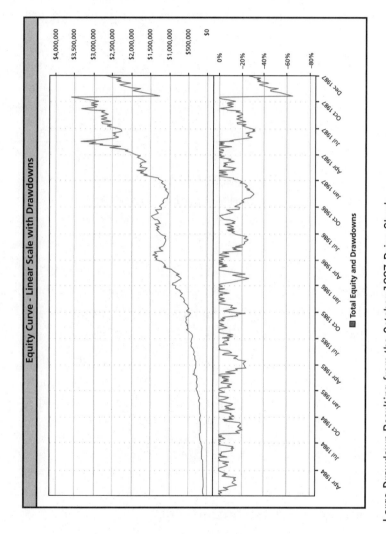

Figure 7-4 Large Drawdown Resulting from the October 1987 Price Shock

the greatest source of anxiety for new traders. They encounter a drawdown and then begin to question their methods: "Did I do something wrong in testing?" "Did the markets change in some way that makes my methods invalid?" "Is this going to continue?"

Ways to mitigate the risk of system death will be discussed in later chapters. Unfortunately, however, since the markets are dynamic and are composed of many other participants, it is a reality that markets change, and this can affect the results of systems and methods that previously worked; sometimes those changes can be permanent. One of the ways great traders distinguish themselves from average traders is by their ability to adhere to methods that others have tired of and discarded and be successful with them.

This consequence that certain market participants stop trading with certain styles because they believe that those styles no longer work has an interesting side effect for trend followers. Every few years trend-following traders experience a period of losses, and inevitably some expert will announce the end of trend following. This usually coincides with a large withdrawal of money from trend-following funds. As more and more money flees from trend-following strategies, those strategies start to become profitable again, often spectacularly so. At least three or four times since the Turtle program began someone has made the claim that trend following has ceased to work. I always laugh at this, knowing that profitable markets are most likely quite near.

Measuring What You Cannot See

There are many ways to quantify risk, which is one way to factor in the pain you would have encountered while trading a particular system. Here are some common measures that I find useful:

1. **Maximum drawdown:** This is a single number that represents the highest percentage loss from peak to subsequent equity low during the course of a test. In Figure 7-4 this would be the 65 percent drawdown that was due to the price shock of the 1987 crash.

2. **Longest drawdown:** The largest period from a peak in equity to a subsequent new peak. This is a measure of how long it would take to regain new equity highs after a losing streak.

3. **Standard deviation of returns:** This is a measure of the dispersion of returns. A low standard deviation of returns indicates that most returns are near the average; a high standard deviation indicates that returns vary more from month to month.

4. **R-squared:** This is a measure of smoothness of fit to the line that represents the CAGR%. A fixed-return investment such as an interest-bearing account would have an R-squared value of 1.0, whereas a very erratic set of returns would have a value lower than 1.0.

The Flip Side of Risk: Rewards

There are many ways to quantify a *reward*, which in the case of a particular trading system relates to the amount of money you might expect to earn when trading that method. Here are some common measures that I find useful:

- **CAGR%:** The compound annual growth rate, also known as the geometric average return, reflects the rate of growth that when compounded equally over the specific period would have resulted in identical ending equity. For simple interest-bearing accounts this is equal to the rate of interest itself. This measure can be affected greatly by a single period of high returns.

- **Average one-year trailing return:** This is the measure of the average return for a rolling one-year period. This measure gives a better sense of what the typical return might be in any specific one-year period. It is relatively less sensitive to a single period of high returns for tests of more than a few years.

- **Average monthly return:** This is the average of each single month's returns over the period of the test.

In addition to these single number measures, I find it useful to examine the equity curve itself as well as a graph that highlights the distribution of monthly returns, as in Figure 4-4 back in Chapter 4. I also like to examine the individual monthly returns over time, as shown in Figure 7-5, which gives the monthly returns for the Donchian Trend system from 1996 to June 2006.

I find that a graph like the one in Figure 7-5 gives a pretty good indication of the relative pain versus reward one can expect and is much more revealing than a single figure or set of figures.

Measuring Risk versus Reward

There are several unified risk/reward measures that are used commonly to compare systems and trading managers who employ systems for their futures trading funds. The most common of these are the Sharpe ratio and the MAR ratio.

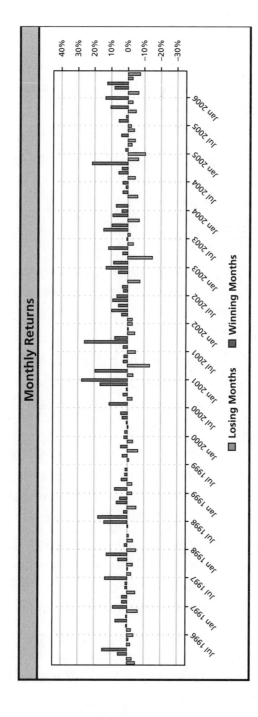

Figure 7-5 Donchian Trend Monthly Returns: January 1996 to June 2006

The Sharpe Ratio

The Sharpe ratio is probably the most common measure used by pension funds and large investors in comparing potential investments. The Sharpe ratio was invented by the Nobel laureate William F. Sharpe in 1966 as a measure for comparing the performance of mutual funds. This measure was introduced as a reward-to-variability ratio but subsequently came to be referred to simply as the Sharpe ratio after its originator.

The Sharpe ratio takes the differential return, which is the CAGR% for the period being measured (i.e., a monthly or yearly period subtracts what is known as the risk-free rate or the rate of interest one could get by investing in a risk-free bond such as a T-bill) and then divides it by the standard deviation of the returns being measured (generally monthly or yearly). Keep in mind that the Sharpe ratio was conceived as a measure for comparing the performance of mutual funds, not as a comprehensive risk/reward measure. Mutual funds are very specific types of investment vehicles that represent an unleveraged investment in a portfolio of stocks.

The original role of the Sharpe ratio as a tool for comparing the performance of mutual funds gives important clues to the types of risks it does not contemplate. Mutual funds as they existed in 1966, when the Sharpe ratio first was proposed, were unleveraged investments in portfolios of U.S. stocks. Thus, a comparison between mutual funds was one between investments in the same markets and with the same basic investment style.

Further, at that time mutual funds held long-term investments in portfolios of stocks. Not having a significant timing or trading component, they differed from each other only in their portfolio selection and diversification strategies. So, for the special case of measuring mutual fund performance, the Sharpe ratio does a very good job of representing that risk because it correctly notes that for comparisons over the same period, the confidence risk relates directly to the variance in the returns. All else being equal, a mutual fund with lower variance has less risk of having a return that deviates from the mean return it exhibited in the past.

Although the Sharpe ratio is an excellent measure of risk/reward in comparing stock portfolio management strategies, it is not a sufficient measure for comparing alternative investment funds such as futures and commodities hedge funds. The Sharpe ratio falls short here because alternative investment funds differ from unleveraged stock portfolios in several important areas that relate to risk:

- **Management style risk:** Futures systems and funds often use short-term trading strategies that can differ greatly from the practices of traditional investment funds that use a buy and hold strategy. It is possible to lose money much more quickly with a trading strategy that involves frequent buying and selling.

- **Diversification strategy risk:** Many futures funds and trading systems do not offer the same level of internal diversification that is found in traditional investments, having a much larger percentage of assets in a small number of instruments at any specific time.

- **Exposure:** Futures have higher leverage than stocks, and this potentially exposes futures traders to more of the risk inherent in market fluctuations.

- **Confidence risk:** Many futures fund managers do not have extensive track records. With a limited track record there is greater risk that an investor will see returns that fall short of expectations.

Unfortunately, the use of the Sharpe ratio tends to exacerbate one of the problems I see in the industry, especially among those who do not understand trading and how it differs from traditional buy-and-hold investment in stocks: The focus on smoothness of returns as a proxy for risk.

Let me be clear as possible here: *Smoothness does not equal risk!* Very risky investments can offer smooth returns for a limited period. Investors tend to believe that an investment or manager who has offered consistent positive returns over a period of several years is a *safe* investment. They hold this belief often without understanding how those returns actually are made.

I believe that there is an *inverse* relationship between smoothness of returns and actual risk in many instances. I offer two examples to support this statement: One concerns a strategy that worked quite well for several years and then stopped working altogether with spectacular results at Long-Term Capital Management; and the second still is employed by many funds that have been delivering excellent returns but have the potential for the same sort of blowup.

When Genius Failed

Long-Term Capital Management (LTCM) used a strategy that relied on very high leverage and the tendency for the price of fixed-income bonds to converge in certain circumstances. Its use of very high leverage caused its positions to become so large relative to the rest of the market that it was very difficult for LTCM to unload those positions when it was faced with losses.

That strategy worked well for several years, but when a financial crisis caused by the Russian default on bonds triggered an adverse price movement, its size worked against LTCM. This occurred because the rest of the market knew that it could keep moving prices against LTCM's positions and that the firm eventually would have to reverse those positions. LTCM ended up losing almost the entire fund, which had been valued at $4.7 billion before the collapse.

Before the crisis, LTCM had averaged almost 40 percent annual returns that were distributed very smoothly. In other words, before that point it had an excellent Sharpe ratio. You can read more about the collapse of Long-Term Capital Management in the book *When Genius Failed* by Roger Lowenstein. (I liked the title so much I was compelled to use it for the heading of this section.)

Not Too Sharp

A similar problem happened recently in natural gas trades at Amaranth, which also built up positions that were very large relative to the rest of the market. Amaranth ended up losing about 65 percent of its $9 billion fund in just two months. Before that it had an excellent Sharpe ratio.

A Brewing Storm?

Currently, there are many hedge funds that achieve returns by selling out of the money options, meaning that they are betting against significant price movement. This can be a very effective strategy that offers particularly smooth returns if the risks are managed properly.

The problem with this approach is that it is difficult for nonprofessionals to understand the actual risks incurred by the funds. It is possible to generate very high and consistent returns by using this strategy while having a very high exposure to any sort of price shock. For example, anyone writing options against the eurodollar in 1987 might have been wiped out. The loss from that price shock combined with the exposure incurred by writing the options could have been enough to result in a single-day loss greater than the value of the fund.

Prudent managers can contain these risks. Unfortunately, many investors find out about these sorts of risks only after it is too late and they have lost their entire investment. They are seduced by the steady returns and multiyear track records of funds that have not yet experienced a truly bad day.

The MAR Ratio

The MAR ratio is a measure that was devised by Managed Accounts Reports, LLC, which reports on the performance of hedge funds. The MAR ratio divides the annual return by the largest drawdown, using month-end figures. This ratio serves as a quick and dirty direct measure of risk/reward that I find very useful for filtering out poorly performing strategies. It is very good for a rough cut. The Donchian Trend system had a MAR ratio of 1.22 over the period tested above from January 1996 to June 2006, where the CAGR% was 27.38 percent and the maximum drawdown using month-end figures was 22.35 percent.

I find the use of month-end figures to be a bit arbitrary and have discovered that it often understates the true drawdown figures; so, in my personal testing I use the maximum drawdown from the peak day to the trough day without regard to where those days fall during the month. To give you some idea of how this might differ from a measure that uses only month-end data, the actual maximum drawdown, including days other than the end of a month, was 27.58 percent rather than 22.35 percent using only month-end figures. The resulting MAR ratio is 0.99 rather than the original 1.22 using only month-end figures.

System Death Risk Revisited

One of the most interesting observations I have made about trading systems, strategies, and performance is that those strategies which historically appear to offer extremely good risk/reward ratios tend to be the ones that are the most heavily imitated by the broader trading community. Soon you end up with billions of dollars in trades chasing that strategy, and as a result, those strategies can implode as they outgrow the liquidity of the markets in which they are traded. They end up suffering from early system death.

Arbitrage strategies are perhaps the best example of this. An arbitrage in its purest form is an essentially risk-free trade. You buy something in one place, sell it at another place, subtract the cost of transportation or storage and pocket the difference. Most arbitrage strategies are not quite that risk-free, but many come close. The problem is that these strategies make money only when there is a spread between the prices at different locations or between the price of one instrument and that of a similar instrument.

The more traders implement a particular strategy, the more the spread will drop as those traders start to compete for essentially the same trades. This effect kills off the strategy over time as it becomes less and less profitable.

Conversely, systems and strategies that do not appeal to the typical investor tend to have much longer lifetimes. Trend following is a good example. Most large investors are uncomfortable with the large drawdowns and equity fluctuations that are common to trend-following strategies. For this reason, trend following continues to work over a long period of time.

Returns tend to be cyclical however. Every time there is a huge new influx of capital after a period of relatively sedate returns, there is generally a period of a few relatively tough years since the market cannot easily digest the amount of new money from investors who are using the same strategies in the same markets. This is generally followed by a period of good returns as investors withdraw their money from trend following funds after periods of relatively poor performance.

Be careful what you look for: If you get too greedy when examining a strategy, you are going to increase the chances that you will not get the results you seek. Strategies that seem to be the best in retrospect are also those most likely to attract new investors and as a consequence often start performing poorly soon after the new investments take place.

Everybody's Different

Each of us has a different tolerance for pain and different expectations for reward. For this reason, there is no single measure that universally appeals to everyone. I have used a combination of the MAR ratio, drawdowns, and overall return while keeping an eye on smoothness by looking at the Sharpe ratio and R-squared figures. Recently I designed some measures that are more stable versions of these common measures. Those measures are discussed in Chapter 12.

I also try not to get too caught up in any particular figures, knowing that the future will be different and that the fact that a strategy has a MAR of 1.5 at the moment does not mean it will continue to maintain that ratio in the future.

RISK AND MONEY
MANAGEMENT

Ruin is the risk you should be concerned with the most.
It can come like a thief in the night and steal everything
if you aren't watching carefully.

Like many of the concepts we use in trading, expectation, edge, risk of ruin and so on, the term *money management* comes from gambling theory. Money management is the art of keeping your risk of ruin at an acceptable level while maximizing your profit potential by choosing an appropriate number of shares or contracts to trade, something we refer to as the *size* of the trade, and by limiting the aggregate size of the position to control exposure to price shocks. Good money management helps ensure that you will continue to be able to trade through the inevitable bad periods that every trader experiences. Most discussions of the topic make use of countless formulas and cover different methods for determining precisely the number of contracts one should trade. They approach risk as if it were a definable and knowable concept, but it isn't. This chapter won't duplicate those discussions. If you want a survey of the many different methods you can use to determine the number of contracts to trade, several books listed in the bibliography cover that topic.

I believe that money management is more art than science, or perhaps more like religion than art. There are no right answers. There are no best ways to define one's risk position. There are only individual answers that work for each person; those answers can be obtained only by asking the right questions.

At its core, money management is about finding the trade-off between taking so much risk that you end up losing everything or are forced to quit trading and, conversely, taking so little risk that you end up leaving too much money on the table. There are two primary ways that excessive risk can force you to stop trading: extended drawdowns that exceed your psychological limits and a sudden price shock that wipes out the account.

Your proper level of risk is very much a function of what is important to you. For that reason, if you want to trade, you have to become intimately familiar with the implications of taking too much risk or too little risk so that you can make an informed decision.

Many vendors of systems or courses on trading make it seem that anyone can follow their methods and achieve riches quickly and easily. They do this because it helps them sell more systems and more courses on trading. They understate the dangers of risk and overstate the probabilities and ease of attaining those riches.

They are lying. *The risk is real, and trading is not easy.*

It is very important to keep one thing in mind before deciding to be aggressive: Steady returns of 20 or 30 percent per year will make you a lot of money in a reasonably short period starting with almost any amount of money. The power of compounding is very strong, but only if you don't lose everything and have to start over again. If you begin with $50,000, you will have almost $10 million after 20 years—if you can earn 30 percent returns.

Trying to go for very aggressive returns of 100 percent or 200 percent per year greatly increases the chances that you will blow up and have to stop trading. I highly recommend taking a conservative approach for the first several years of trading.

Consider what would have happened if you had been trading with the Donchian Trend system in 1987 at aggressive levels. Figure 8-1 shows the drawdowns that are encountered as the risk levels increase.

Note how the graph rises steadily and levels off at the 100 percent point. This means that if you were trading aggressively and risking 3 percent of your trading capital on each trade, you would have gone bust overnight because this drawdown is due entirely to that single day when the interest-rate markets reversed precipitously.

For most people, a prudent way to trade would be at a level that demonstrates a drawdown, using historical simulations, that is at most one-half the level you believe you can tolerate. This will provide a buffer in case the system has a drawdown that is larger than what previously had been seen during testing. It also will make it less likely that an unexpected price shock will cause you to lose all your trading capital.

Don't Believe Everything You Hear

Many people have touted money management as a magical elixir that can cure all that ails your trading. Others have devised com-

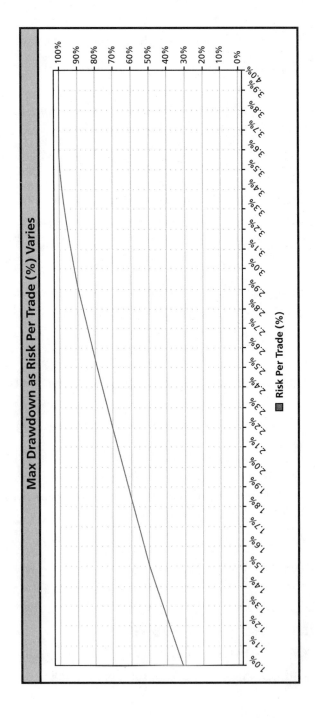

Figure 8-1   Drawdown versus Risk

plex formulas and written entire books about money management. It shouldn't be that complicated.

Proper money management is quite simple. For a trading account of a particular size, you can safely buy a certain number of contracts in each futures market. For some markets and for smaller accounts this amount may be zero.

For example, the natural gas (NYMEX symbol NG) contract earlier this year had an ATR that represented more than $7,500 per contract. Remember, this means that the value of the contract fluctuated $7,500 on the average each day. Thus, for a system that used a 2-ATR stop such as the Donchian Trend system, a single trade could mean a loss of $15,000. If you were trading an account as large as $50,000, this would represent 30 percent of the account. Most people would say that risking 30 percent of your trading account on one trade is a really bad idea. Therefore, a prudent number of contracts of NG to trade would be zero for an account of $50,000. Even for an account as large as $1 million, such a trade would represent a 1.5 percent risk level, which many would consider fairly aggressive.

Trading with too much risk is probably the single most common reason for failure among new traders. Often novices trade so aggressively that a small string of losses will wipe out their trading capital. New traders often misunderstand the dangers of leverage, and because their broker and the exchange permits them to buy and sell large contracts with as little as $20,000, they often do precisely that.

Risk of Ruin Revisited

Earlier we discussed the concept of risk of ruin: The possibility of losing so much capital as a result of a string of losses that one is forced to quit trading. The definition as most people use it applies to a random set of outcomes using a fairly simplistic formula based on probability theory. Most people think in terms of the risk that you will experience ruin due to a bad period of losses in rapid succession. I believe that this is not generally what brings traders to ruin. Traders do not fall prey to a period of randomly adverse market behavior very often. It is far more likely that they have made some serious mistakes in their analysis.

Here is what I believe accounts for a trader's lack of success in trading commodities:

- **No plan:** Many traders base their trades on hunches, rumor, guesses, and the belief that they know something about the future direction of prices.

- **Too much risk:** Many otherwise excellent traders have been ruined because they incurred too much risk. I'm not talking about 50 percent or 100 percent more risk than is prudent. I have seen traders who trade at a level that is 5 or 10 times more than I consider prudent even for aggressive trading.

- **Unrealistic expectations:** Many new traders trade with too much risk because they have unrealistic expectations about how much they can earn and what sorts of returns they can achieve. This is often also the reason new traders believe they can start trading on the basis of fundamental data; they believe they are smart enough to "beat" the market with little or no training and very little information.

When I started working with futures trading systems in high school, I noticed something rather odd: A very high percentage of

MAKE A PLAN

our customers were doctors and dentists. At the time, I believed that doctors and dentists were attracted to trading because they had good incomes and could afford to risk money in futures markets. Looking back on it, I can see that was only a partial answer. I now believe that the real reason doctors and dentists are drawn in disproportionate numbers to commodities trading is that they have a lot of confidence in their intelligence and ability to translate their success in their work to success in another industry—perhaps too much confidence in this particular instance.

A doctor, for example, is invariably quite smart. You can't become a doctor without attending a good university, passing difficult tests, and getting good grades. Further, anyone who has graduated from medical school has achieved a level of success that many aspire to but only a few attain. It must be quite natural for someone who is smart and has been successful in his first endeavors to believe that he can be successful at trading as well.

At the same time, many doctors and dentists expect to be successful traders immediately. Trading appears to be so simple that they believe that this should be possible. However, I found that a large percentage of them were not successful as traders because they did not have realistic expectations. Success in one sphere of business does not guarantee success in trading.

They did not realize that although trading is simple for the reasons I outlined in the early part of the book, it is *not* easy. It takes a lot of time and study before one realizes just how simple trading is, but it takes many years of failure before most traders come to grips with how hard it can be to keep things simple and not lose sight of the basics.

Consider the Turtles. We were taught the same methods and taught in only two weeks, yet some of us did not make any money at all. There was lots of positive reinforcement to do the right thing since we could hear the other Turtles phoning in orders, yet some of us did not follow the methods we were taught.

Turtle Money Management
Means Staying in the Game

The primary goal of trading should be to stay in the game. Time is on your side. A system or method with positive expectation eventually will make you rich, sometimes beyond your wildest dreams. This can happen only if you can continue trading. For traders, death comes in two forms: a slow painful death that causes traders to stop out of anguish and frustration and a spectacular rapid death we refer to as a *blowup*.

Most new traders overestimate their tolerance for pain, believing that they can live through a 30 percent or 40 percent—or perhaps even a 50 percent or 70 percent—drawdown when they can't. This can have an extremely adverse effect on their trading because it usually results in their stopping completely or changing methods at the worst possible time: After they have incurred a drawdown and suffered significant losses.

The uncertainty of the future is what makes trading so difficult, and people do not like uncertainty. Unfortunately, the reality is that the markets *are* unpredictable and the best you can hope for is a method that generally works over a relatively long period. For this reason, your trading methods should be designed as much as possible to reduce the uncertainty you can expect to encounter when trading. The markets are already uncertain enough; there is no sense adding to that variability with poor money management practices.

Since the Turtle Way is not to predict which markets will trend and which trades will be successful, as Turtles we approached each trade with the same expectation and commitment. To the extent possible, that meant risking the same amount of capital in each market. Implementing money management according to the Turtle Way increases the likelihood that you will achieve consistent returns because our approach adjusts for the relative volatility and risk between markets.

Oversimplified strategies such as trading one contract per market and methods that do not normalize for volatility can cause trades in certain markets to overshadow those in other markets. So, even a *large gain* in one market may not compensate for a *small loss* in another market if the losing market has a much larger contract.

Although many traders intuitively know this is true, many still use fairly simplistic mechanisms for deciding how many contracts to trade in any specific market. For example, they may trade one contract of S&P 500 futures per $20,000 in the trading account. They may have used this same formula for the last 10 years, during which time that market's volatility has fluctuated greatly. These rule-of-thumb approaches can increase the variability of returns unnecessarily.

The *N* Factor

As was mentioned earlier, Rich and Bill used an innovative method for determining the position size for each market on the basis of the amount that market moved up and down each day in constant dollar terms. They determined the number of contracts for each market that would cause them all to move up and down approximately the same amount in dollar terms. Since the number of contracts we traded for each market was adjusted for this volatility measure, N, the daily fluctuations for any particular trade tended to be similar.

Some traders prefer to measure risk in terms of the distance between the price at which one will exit a trade and the price at which that trade was entered. That is only one way of considering risk. In October 1987, it did not matter where our stops had been. The market gapped through our stops overnight.

If I had been using a method that relied only on the distance between entry and stops, I would have lost four times as much as the typical Turtle on that day because I used a stop that was one-quarter the size. I used a ½-ATR stop, whereas most Turtles used a 2-ATR stop. Thus, if I had been using a method that sized purely on the distance to the stop, my calculations would have resulted in a position that was four times larger than that of the typical Turtle.

Fortunately, Rich used volatility-based position sizing as a way to manage risk, and so I had the same position sizes relative to my account as did the other Turtles, and our exposure to the price shock was the same. I am certain that this method was not accidental. Surely Rich and Bill both recalled experiencing prior price shocks when they determined how to limit the Turtles' maximum allowable risk levels.

One of the smartest things Rich and Bill did when they gave us our trading rules was to impose overall risk limits on us. This had important implications for our drawdowns and particularly for our exposure to price shocks. As was mentioned earlier, we put our positions in chunks we called units. Each unit was sized by determining the number of contracts where 1-ATR of price movement would be equal to 1 percent of our account size. For a $1 million trading account, this was $10,000. So, we would look at the dollar amount represented by 1-ATR of price movement in that particular market and then divide $10,000 by that number to determine the number of contracts we could trade for every $1 million in trading capital that Rich had allocated to us. We referred to these numbers as the *unit size*. Markets that were volatile or had larger contracts had smaller unit sizes than did markets that were smaller or less volatile.

Rich and Bill no doubt had noticed some things that anyone who has traded for a period of time is aware of: Many markets are highly correlated, and at the end of a large trend when the bad days come, it seems that everything moves against you at once; even markets that normally do not seem correlated become so on those volatile days when a large trend disintegrates.

Recall the October 1987 overnight price shock. Almost every market we were in moved against us significantly that day. To counter that effect, Rich and Bill imposed some limits on our trading: First, we could put on a maximum of only 4 units per market; second, we could put on a maximum of only 6 units in markets that were highly correlated; third, we could put on a maximum of only 10 units in any given direction (i.e., 10 long or 10 short). That number could be raised to 12 if there were positions in uncorrelated markets. These limits probably saved Rich more than $100 million that day. If they had not been in place, our losses would have been staggering.

I often have seen people claim to have tested the historical performance of the Turtle system and state that those methods did not work well or were not profitable. They would make statements such as: "I implemented every rule except the unit limits." The unit limits were an integral and extremely important part of our system because they served as a mechanism for filtering out trades in lagging markets.

Interest-rate futures provide a good example. We traded four different interest-rate markets as Turtles: eurodollars, U.S. Treasury bonds, 90-day Treasury bills, and two-year Treasury notes. During a move of any reasonable duration there would be entry signals in all four markets. We generally would hold positions in only two of them at any specific time: The first two that had signaled.

The same thing generally held for foreign currency futures. We traded the French franc, the British pound, the German mark, the Swiss franc, the Canadian dollar, and the Japanese yen. However, at any given time we typically would have a position in only two or perhaps three of those markets.

For this reason, having unit limits kept us out of a lot of losing trades. The markets that signaled last often did not move nearly as far and were more likely to result in losses.

Rules for Estimating Risk

One of the best ways to determine the risk a particular system may represent or the risk inherent in holding a position is to look at the major price shocks that have occurred over the last 30 to 50 years. If you look at those catastrophic days and consider what would have happened to a set of likely positions, you can determine what amount of risk would have resulted in a 50 percent drawdown or the amount it would have taken to go completely bust. Using computer simulation software, it is easy to see what positions you would have held on those days and what sort of drawdowns are represented by those positions.

Now consider what would happen if something even worse had occurred. It may be unpleasant to think about such things, but they can happen, and you need to plan for them. What would have happened to your positions if instead of their attack on the World Trade Center, al-Qaeda had detonated a nuclear bomb somewhere else in Manhattan? What would have happened if a disaster of equal magnitude had taken place in Tokyo, London, or Frankfurt?

Anyone trading aggressively will be much more likely to lose everything in the event of a disaster of unprecedented scale. This is something to keep in mind as you hear the siren call of 100 percent-plus returns.

nine

TURTLE-STYLE
BUILDING BLOCKS

*Don't spend all your time admiring the fancy tools
in the magazines. First learn how to use the basic ones well.
It's not the size of your tools that counts but how well you use them.*

Chapter 2 provided an overview of the various market states: stable and quiet, stable and volatile, trending and quiet, and trending and volatile. I also pointed out the importance of being able to identify the state of the market you are trading in since many systems are designed to keep you out of that market when it's in a state that is not favorable given their trading styles.

I refer to the tools that indicate market states as *building blocks*. Some building blocks have specific names such as *indicators, oscillators,* and *ratios,* but I group them all into the more general category. This chapter focuses on the building blocks for trend-following systems. These are tools that indicate when the market may have moved from a stable state to a trending state and, conversely, when it has moved back to a stable state. Simply put, they indicate when a trend may have started and when it may have ended.

Unfortunately for traders, there are no building blocks that work all the time, no secret formulas that lead to an easy fortune. The best we can do is find tools that help us identify times when the odds that a trend has started or ended have improved. This is sufficient for our purposes since it is possible to make good returns even when the odds are only slightly in your favor (ask your favorite casino owner).

One Brick at a Time

Let's begin with a survey of many common trend-following building blocks, including the ones we were taught in the Turtle program. These are ways to determine when a trend may be starting and when it may have ended. This is not a complete survey: You can find entire books that do nothing more than outline different indicators and system rules that can be used to build trend-following systems. For other types of trading there are other types of building blocks that may be useful. Since this book is not a comprehensive treatise, however, I'll leave the discovery of those tools as an exercise for the reader. The building blocks discussed in this chapter are the following:

- **Breakouts:** These are situations when the price exceeds the highest high or the lowest low for a specific number of days. This was the primary tool used in the original Turtle system.
- **Moving averages:** These are continuously calculated averages of the price for a specific number of days. They are called moving averages because they are calculated each day and their value therefore moves up and down with the new prices.

- **Volatility channels:** These are built by adding a specific amount of price to a moving average that is based on a measure of market volatility such as the standard deviation or ATR.

- **Time-based exits:** These are the simplest possible exits: You exit the market at a specific, predetermined time (e.g., exit the market after 10 days or after 80 days).

- **Simple lookbacks:** These involve a comparison of the current price with a historical price at some earlier period.

We will explore each building block in more detail and demonstrate how it can be used in a trend-following system.

Breakouts

Earlier in the book I discussed breakouts and showed how they have an edge. A new high price is a strong indicator of the possibility that a trend is beginning. The number of days used to calculate the highest high or the lowest low for the breakout will determine the type of trend you may be entering. Fewer days will indicate the possibility of a shorter-term trend. A large number of days will be more indicative of the possibility of a longer-term trend. Breakouts work especially well when they are combined with other indicators of overall trend, such as the Donchian Trend system, which uses breakouts for both entry signals and exit signals and moving averages to indicate the overall trend.

Moving Averages

Moving averages are continuously calculated averages of the price for a specific number of days. The simplest type of moving average,

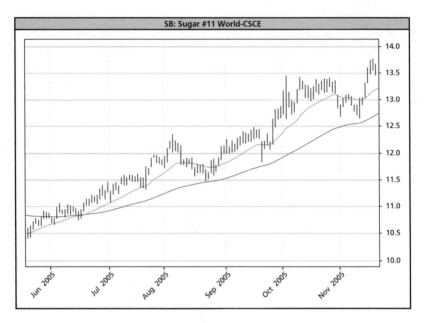

Figure 9-1 20-Day and 70-Day Exponential Moving Averages

Copyright 2006 Trading Blox, LLC. All rights reserved worldwide.

called a *simple moving* average, is the average of the price for a specified number of days. The 10-day moving average of the close is the average of the prior 10 days' closes, and a 70-day moving average of the high is the average of the previous 70 highs.

There are other kinds of moving averages that are slightly more complex, the most common being the *exponential moving average*. This is an average that is computed by taking a portion of the previous day's average and mixing it with a portion of the current price. Figure 9-1 presents two moving averages: a 20-day exponential moving average and a 70-day exponential moving average.

You can see how the 20-day moving average follows the price more closely and how it crosses the longer-term moving average in mid-June, indicating the start of an up trend. This is a very common system entry: A trade is taken in the direction of the shorter moving average when it crosses over the longer moving average. In this case, a long trade would have been initiated in early June at the point of the crossover.

Many other different types of moving averages have been proposed by system designers and researchers. Most of the additional complexity offered by their designers is not all that useful in actual practice and presents a greater potential for curve fitting and unrealistic test results. This potential pitfall is considered in greater detail in Chapter 11.

Volatility Channels

Volatility channels are good indicators of the beginning of a trend. If the price exceeds a particular moving average plus some additional amount, this means that the price is going up. In other words, it indicates that a trend possibly has begun. We will examine two different systems built on volatility channels in Chapter 10.

Figure 9-2 shows an 80-day moving average with a volatility channel plotted both above and below the moving average. You can see from the graph that the prices remain inside the channel for the most part except in the right-hand part of the graph, when they descend below the channel. You also can see how the moving average slowly turns down and follows the prices as they go lower.

Time-Based Exits

A simple time-based exit can be very effective and useful. It also can help smooth out the drawdowns associated with a breakdown in a trend. This is the case because very often a time-based exit

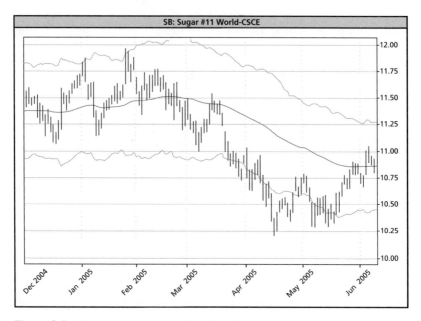

Figure 9-2 Moving Average with Volatility Channel

Copyright 2006 Trading Blox, LLC. All rights reserved worldwide.

occurs before the drawdown is revealed by a moving average or breakout, both of which follow price more closely.

Simple Lookbacks

If you consider at a very basic level what trend following is, you can devise even simpler mechanisms for determining the potential start of a trend. One method that works reasonably well is to simply look at a price some number of days earlier. You can add those prices by using a volatility-based measure such as ATR. For example, you can buy if the prices exceed the price 100 days ago by 2 ATR.

Chapter 10 will explore some systems that use other types of simple lookbacks.

Want More?

Over the years, hundreds of different types of indicators have been invented. Recently, advances in technology have made it easier for traders to program their own formulas and create their own indicators, and trading magazines publish new indicators and systems built on those indicators in each new issue. For those who want to learn about other indicators and system building blocks in more detail, some sources are included in the bibliography. However, before you dig in too deeply, here are some words of advice. I'll use trend following as an example, but this advice applies to other types of trading as well.

If a market starts to go up, sooner or later it will trigger a long entry signal using any of the trend-following building blocks. All the building blocks can be tuned so that they react more quickly or more slowly. Therefore, in effect you can use any of them to build systems that will perform similarly to systems built with other building blocks.

My advice is that there are better ways to spend your time than searching for the perfect newfangled nuclear-powered indicator that works perfectly in past years' markets. I suggest that instead you try out some simple systems that use the basic building blocks that were outlined above. We will look at some of them in Chapter 10.

TURTLE-STYLE TRADING: STEP BY STEP

*Keep it simple. Simple time-tested methods that are
well executed will beat fancy complicated methods every time.*

This chapter will look at some Turtle-style trading systems, more commonly known as long-term trend-following systems. Those systems are as follows:

- **ATR Channel Breakout:** A volatility channel system that uses ATR as the volatility measure.

- **Bollinger Breakout:** A volatility channel system that uses the standard deviation as the volatility measure.

- **Donchian Trend:** A breakout system with a trend filter.

- **Donchian Trend with Time Exit:** A breakout system with a trend filter and a time-based exit.

- **Dual Moving Average:** A system that buys and sells when a faster moving average crosses over a slower moving average. Unlike the other systems, this system is always in the market, either long or short.

- **Triple Moving Average:** A system that buys and sells when a faster moving average crosses over a slower moving average but only in the direction of the major trend defined by a very slow-moving average.

To examine the differences among these systems, I ran a series of historical simulations to determine how much money one would have made if one had used each of those systems for the last ten years. This chapter will use some of the metrics discussed in Chapter 7 to compare the relative performance of each of the systems.

To Test or Not to Test

There are many traders, including quite a few successful ones, who do not believe in historical testing, sometimes referred to as *backtesting*. They believe that testing with historical data is not useful because the past will not repeat itself. For readers who are not familiar with this debate, I am going to spend several paragraphs convincing you of something that you probably think needs no explanation. To those who do not believe in historical testing, my question is: What is the alternative? How do you arrive at any strategy without knowledge of the past? How do you determine when to buy or sell? Do you guess?

The only information you have is what the markets have done so far. Even if you are a discretionary trader who does not use rules or systems, you still have your personal experience of historical price action as a guide. You are relying on your interpretation of the past; in effect you are relying on historical data.

Smart discretionary traders can develop systems after years of experience in trading. They note repeating patterns that offer opportunities for profits. They then trade by using ideas designed to capitalize on those opportunities. New traders often pore over charts for months before starting to trade so that they can understand what the market did in the past. They do this because they know that the best indication of what the markets are likely to do in the future is contained in the past.

It is not hard to argue that computers can test ideas more reliably using the same historical data. Computer simulation enables traders to perform a more rigorous analysis of a particular strategy before trading begins. Then the traders often find that ideas that appeared promising will not work because of something that was not anticipated. It is much better to figure this out by computer than with an actual account.

The reason some traders do not believe in historical simulation is that there are many ways to distort backtesting. It is easy to use the power of a computer to find methods that appear to work but will not work in real markets. These problems are tractable if you make sure to avoid the most common pitfall: Overoptimization. This topic is covered in Chapter 11.

Proper historical testing requires some experience and skills that beginning traders do not possess. However, the fact that you would not give a sharp knife to a small child does not mean you don't want to use one in the kitchen when you are cooking. You just need to be careful with sharp instruments.

A historical simulation does not predict what you will encounter in future trading, but it will give you a way to determine whether an approach is likely to be profitable in the future. It is not the optimal solution—a crystal ball or time machine would be better—but it is the best tool that is currently available.

The Myth of the Expert

The "don't optimize" counsel is an effect of what my friends and I like to call the myth of the expert. Unfortunately, in most fields the number of people who really understand what's going on is very limited. For every true expert, there are scores of *pseudo-experts* who are able to perform in the field, have assembled loads of knowledge, and in the eyes of those who are not experts are indistinguishable from the true experts. These pseudo-experts can function but do not really *understand* the area in which they claim expertise.

True experts do not have rigid rules; they *understand* what's going on, and so they do not need rigid rules.

Pseudo-experts, however, *don't understand*, and so they tend to look at what the experts are doing and copy it. They know *what to do* but not *why it should be done*. Therefore, they listen to the true experts and create rigid rules where none were intended.

One sure sign of a pseudo-expert is writing that is unclear and difficult to follow. Unclear writing comes from unclear thinking. A true expert will be able to explain complicated ideas in ways that are clear and easy to understand.

Another common characteristic of pseudo-experts is that they know how to apply complex processes and techniques and have been well trained but do not understand the limits of those techniques.

In trading, a good example would be someone who can perform complex statistical analyses of trades, runs a simulation that generates 1,000 trades, and then assumes that she can draw conclusions from those trades without regard for the fact that they might have been drawn from only two weeks of short-term data. These people can do the math but do not understand that the math does not matter if next week is radically different from the last two weeks.

Don't confuse experience with expertise or knowledge with wisdom.

Common Building Blocks

The testing described in this chapter was performed using a common portfolio of markets and a common money management algorithm to keep the differences in results isolated to those effects which are due to changes in the rules of the system. Here are the variables used in the testing discussed in this chapter.

Markets

The markets in the testing portfolio include the Australian dollar, the British pound, corn, cocoa, the Canadian dollar, crude oil, cotton, the euro, the eurodollar, feeder cattle, gold, copper, heating oil, unleaded gas, the Japanese yen, coffee, cattle, hogs, the Mexican peso, natural gas, soybeans, sugar, the Swiss franc, silver, Treasury notes, Treasury bonds, and wheat.

These markets were selected from the liquid (high-trading-volume) U.S. markets. A few liquid markets were eliminated because they were very highly correlated with other, more liquid markets. We decided to limit our testing for these purposes to U.S. markets because many of the providers of historical data sell the information for foreign markets separately. For that reason, many new traders start with the U.S. markets only, and we wanted to make it as easy as possible for traders to duplicate our results in their own testing.

Money Management

The money management algorithm used here was the same as that used by the Turtles except that we employed a figure that was half as aggressive. Instead of equating 1 ATR to 1 percent of our trading equity, we equated it to 0.5 percent. To arrive at number of contracts for the test, we divided 0.5 percent of the equity by the value of a given market's ATR in terms of dollars at the point when the orders were entered for a specific trade.

Test Dates

The testing was performed using data from January 1996 through June 2006 for all the systems.

The Systems

Let's examine each system in greater detail before revealing the testing results.

ATR Channel Breakout

The ATR Channel Breakout system is a volatility channel system that uses the average true range as the volatility measure. The channel is formed by adding 7 ATR to a 350-day moving average of the closing prices for the channel top and subtracting 3 ATR from the moving average for the channel bottom. A long trade is entered on the open if the previous day's close exceeded the top of the channel; a short trade is entered if the previous day's close fell below the bottom of the channel. Trades are exited when the close crosses back through the moving average price.

A variation of the ATR Channel Breakout system was popularized as the PGO (Pretty Good Oscillator) system by the trader Mark

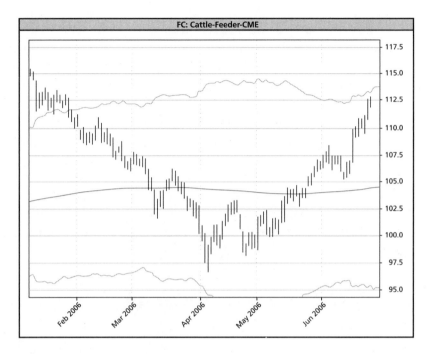

Figure 10-1 ATR Channel Breakout System

Johnson on Chuck LeBeau's System Trader's Club (www. traderclub.com) forum. It is also a variant of the Bollinger Breakout system discussed below. Figure 10-1 shows a graph of the volatility channel for the ATR Channel Breakout system.

The middle line is the 350-day moving average, and the top line is the top of the volatility channel formed by adding 7 ATR to the moving average.

Bollinger Breakout

This system was described by Chuck LeBeau and David Lucas in their 1992 book *Technical Traders Guide to Computer Analysis of the Futures Markets* (using different numbers for the days in the moving average and the standard deviations for the channel width). A Bollinger band is a volatility channel that was invented by John Bollinger. The Bollinger band for this system is formed by adding and subtracting 2.5 standard deviations of the close to a 350-day moving average. A long trade is entered on the open if the previous day's close exceeded the top of the channel; a short trade is entered if the previous day's close fell below the bottom of the channel. Trades are exited when the close crosses back through the moving average price. Figure 10-2 shows a graph of the volatility channel for the Bollinger Breakout system.

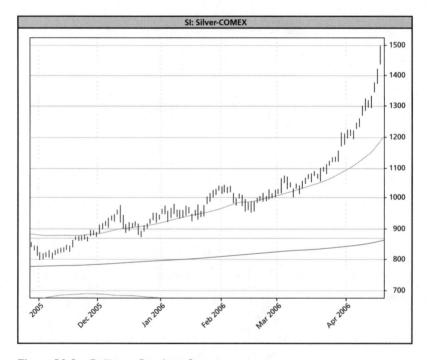

Figure 10-2   Bollinger Breakout System

Donchian Trend

This Donchian Trend system, which was described in Chapter 5, is a simplified version of the system we used as Turtles. It uses a 20-day breakout for entry and a 10-day breakout for exits and includes a 350-day/25-day exponential moving average trend filter. Trades are taken only in the direction indicated by the faster moving average. If the 25-day moving average is above the 350-day average, only longs may be taken; if the 25-day moving average is below the 350-day average, only shorts may be taken. The system also uses a 2-ATR stop just as the original Turtle system did. Figure 10-3 shows the breakout levels and moving averages for the Donchian Trend system.

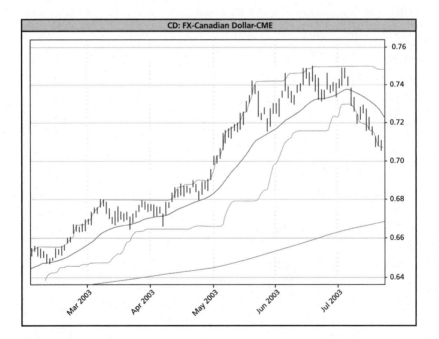

Figure 10-3   Donchian Trend System

The smooth line that follows the prices fairly closely is the short moving average; the lower smooth line at the bottom is the long moving average. The graph indicates that a long-trend is in progress, and so only long trades will be taken. The jagged lines at the top and bottom of the prices are the breakout levels. The highest high moves directly as a new high is made, and so it closely follows the price on the way up. Note that the lowest low does not follow the price as closely as the price moves up.

The chart shows that a long trade would have been entered on April 10 as the price penetrated the former highest high at 0.6802, which had been made on March 7. Note too how a previous attempt to exceed that price at the end of March was unsuccessful. This is a good example of resistance indicating selling. The second time the price rose to that level, it was able to break through and rally 6 cents to 0.74 without any significant pullbacks. The price was able to rise because there were no more traders willing to sell at that level but there were buyers willing to buy at the higher prices.

Donchian Trend with Time Exit

A variation on the Donchian Trend system, the *Donchian Trend with Time Exit* system, uses a time-based exit instead of a breakout exit. It exits the trade after 80 days and does not use any stops whatsoever. There are many traders who state that entries do not matter; only exits do. This system is my response to that statement. When we compare the performance of this system with that of the other systems, you will be able to see how this very simple exit compares with more sophisticated exits.

Dual Moving Average

This is a very simple system that buys and sells when a 100-day moving average crosses over a slower 350-day moving average. Unlike the other systems, this system is always in the market, either long or short. The only time a trade is exited is when the fast-moving average crosses over, at which time the trade is exited and a new trade is initiated in the opposite direction. Figure 10-4 shows the moving averages for the Dual Moving Average system.

The 100-day moving average more closely follows the price, and when it crosses it at the end of July, a long trade will be entered. As you probably can tell, this system is a very long term trend-following

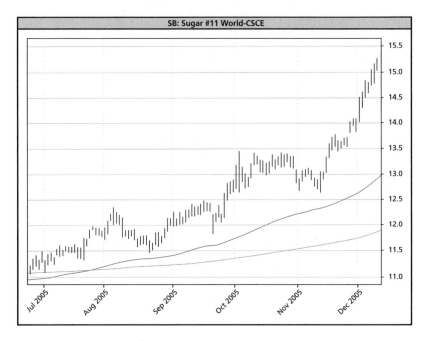

Figure 10-4   Dual Moving Average System

system and does not trade all that often compared with most other systems.

Triple Moving Average

This system uses three moving averages: a 150-day average, a 250-day average, and a 350-day average. The buys and sells occur when the 150-day moving average crosses over a slower 250-day moving average. The system uses the longer 350-day average as a trend filter. Trades happen only when both moving averages are on the same side as the longer 350-day average. If both are higher, long trades are permitted; if both are lower, only short trades are permitted.

Unlike the Dual Moving Average system, this system is not always in the market. Trades are exited when the 150-day average crosses the 250-day average. Figure 10-5 illustrates the moving averages for the Triple Moving Average system.

The top line is the 150-day average, the middle line is the 250-day average, and the lower line is the 350-day average. You can see how all three lines slowly follow the price upward on this chart, which uses the same time period as the one in Figure 10-4. The system will exit the trade when the top line crosses back under the middle line.

Before we move on to the next section, guess what the relative performance of these systems for the period indicated will be. How much worse will the time-based exit be than the normal breakout exit? Which two systems do you guess will have the best MAR ratio? How much better will the Triple Moving Average system perform than the Dual Moving Average system?

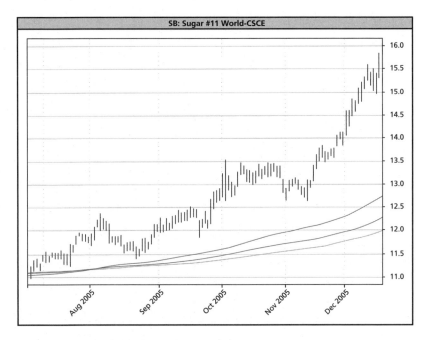

Figure 10-5 Triple Moving Average System

The Results Are In

I tested all six systems with the same test data—money management, portfolio, and test start and stop dates—using our trading simulation software, Trading Blox Builder. The software ran a simulation for each of the systems from January 1996 through June 2006. It simulated every trade and generated performance statistics for each of the systems. Table 10-1 shows some of the most common performance metrics for each of the six systems.

Table 10-1 Historical System Performance Comparison

System	CAGR%	MAR	Sharpe	Trades	W%	Max DD	DD Length
ATR CBO	49.5%	1.24	1.34	206	42.2%	39.9%	8.3
Bollinger CBO	51.8%	1.52	1.52	130	54.6%	34.1%	7.8
Donchian Trend	29.4%	0.80	0.99	1.832	39.7%	36.7%	27.6
Donchian Time	57.2%	1.31	1.35	746	58.3%	43.6%	12.1
Dual MA	57.8%	1.82	1.55	210	39.5%	31.8%	8.3
Triple MA	48.1%	1.53	1.37	181	42.5%	31.3%	8.5

Source: Copyright 2006 Trading Blox, LLC. All rights reserved worldwide.
Note: Channel Breakout is abbreviated as CBO and Moving Average is abbreviated as MA, Drawdown as DD, Maximum as Max, and Winning Percentage as W% in 10-1 and other tables in this book.

When I first tested the time-based exits, I was floored. They performed far better than I had imagined they would, better even than the breakout-based exits. So much for the idea that it is the exit that makes a system profitable. This shows that an entry that has an edge can account for the entire profitability of a system.

Note also how the Donchian system did not perform as well as the other systems. This highlights how breakouts have lost some of their edge in the years since the Turtle program. I believe this is largely due to what I describe in the Chapter 11 as *trader effects*.

The other notable surprise in Table 10-1 is the performance of the Dual Moving Average system, which demonstrated better performance than did its more complex counterpart the Triple Moving Average System. This is just one example of many that suggest that the fact that a system is complex does not necessarily make it better.

All of these are basic systems. Three of them—the Dual Moving Average system, the Triple Moving Average system, and the Donchian

Trend with time-based exit system—do not even have any stops. This means that they violate one of the most cherished maxims of trading—"Always have a stop loss"—yet their risk-adjusted performance is as good as or better than that of the other systems.

Adding Stops

Many traders are uncomfortable with the idea of having absolutely no stops. What do you think will happen to the performance of the Dual Moving Average system if we add stops? Many people like to speculate about these sorts of things. They ask their friends or go to more experienced traders with their questions.

I prefer to try out an idea and benefit from the confidence that comes from having concrete answers. Figure 10-6 demonstrates the effect of using a stop at various widths in ATR from the point of entry.

Note that the zero case, which means no stop at all, has the best MAR ratio numbers. In fact, the test with no stops is better for all the metrics: CAGR%, MAR ratio, Sharpe ratio, drawdown, and length of drawdown—every single metric. The same thing holds true for a test of the Triple Moving Average system: Every single measure was worse with any stops. The same test of stops applied to the Donchian Trend with time-based exit system yields similar results except that for very large stops of 10 ATR or more, the results are about the same as those for a test with no stops. This certainly goes against the common belief that one must always have a stop. Why is this? Weren't we taught that stops are very important for preserving capital? How come the drawdowns do not go down when we add stops?

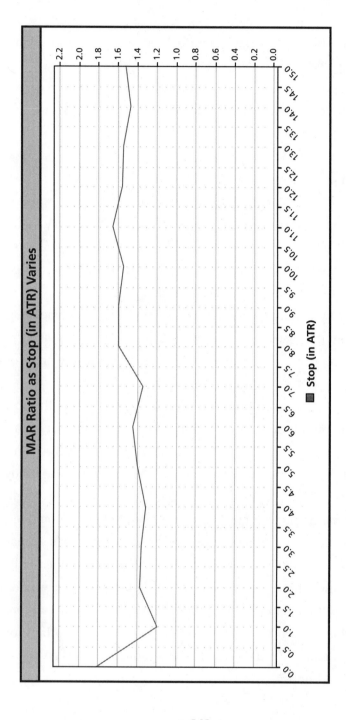

Figure 10-6 Effect of Stops on the Dual Moving Average System

Many traders believe that what they need to worry about is the risk of a series of losing trades. Although this may be true for short-term traders who have trades that last for a few days, it is not true for trend followers. For trend followers, drawdowns also come from trend reversals, usually after major trends. Sometimes the trend reversals are followed by very volatile markets in which it can be extremely difficult to trade.

We Turtles knew that giving up part of the profits we had accumulated during a trend is a normal part of trading as a trend follower. We knew that we would experience large drawdowns. Nevertheless, this was really painful for some of the Turtles, especially the ones who were the most affected by losing money. Watching profits vanish after they have just been earned is the hardest part of our style of trading.

Thus, it is not entry risk that causes drawdowns for trend followers; it is giving back profits. This will be covered more extensively Chapter 11, but first let's return to testing the systems.

The Results Are In Again

Recall that the systems were tested through the end of June 2006, and as I write this, many more months have passed. You may be curious about what happened to our systems in the interim.

Which system would you have picked to trade based on the data through June 2006? If you could have chosen two systems, which ones would you have picked? I changed the end date for the tests, using data through the end of November 2006, and Table 10-2 shows the updated results.

Table 10-2   Historical System Performance Comparison through November 2006

System	CAGR%	MAR	Sharpe	Trades	W%	Max DD	DD Length
ATR CBO	45.9%	1.15	1.27	216	43.1%	40.0%	8.3
Bollinger CBO	49.2%	1.44	1.47	136	53.7%	34.1%	7.8
Donchian Trend	27.4%	0.75	0.94	1901	38.7%	38.7%	27.6
Donchian Time	57.1%	1.31	1.34	773	59.1%	43.6%	12.1
Dual MA	49.1%	1.04	1.34	222	36.9%	47.2%	8.3
Triple MA	41.2%	0.97	1.21	186	41.9%	42.3%	8.5

Source: Copyright 2006 Trading Blox, LLC. All rights reserved worldwide.

A quick glance at the CAGR% and MAR ratio tells you fairly quickly that the last few months of 2006 were bad for trend-following systems in general. The interesting aspect here is the changes that occurred. Table 10-3 reveals the percentage changes in CAGR% and maximum drawdown.

Table 10-3   Comparative Performance through June 2006 versus through November 2006

System	CAGR% 11/06	CAGR% 06/06	Δ%	Max DD 11/06	Max DD 06/06	Δ%
ATR CBO	45.9%	49.5%	−7.3%	40.0%	39.9%	0.3%
Bollinger CBO	49.2%	51.8%	−5.0%	34.1%	34.1%	0.0%
Donchian Trend	27.4%	29.4%	−6.8%	38.7%	36.7%	5.4%
Donchian Time	57.1%	57.2%	−0.2%	43.6%	43.6%	0.0%
Dual MA	49.1%	57.8%	−15.1%	47.2%	31.8%	48.4%
Triple MA	41.2%	48.1%	−14.3%	42.3%	31.3%	35.1%

Source: Copyright 2006 Trading Blox, LLC. All rights reserved worldwide.

What happened? How did our results change so dramatically? Why did our best system have a 50 percent increase in the size of the drawdown? Why did the system that used the simplest exit have no change in performance over the last five months when some other systems did especially poorly? How does a trader build systems that are more likely to perform to expectations? Put a different way, how can you conform your expectations to better fit the probable outcomes of trading a system?

These questions offer an apt introduction to Chapter 11, which will examine all these issues and increase your understanding of the difference between the results you might get in a backtest and what you might expect in actual trading, as well as those factors which influence the disparity between tested and actual trading results.

LIES, DAMN LIES, AND BACKTESTS

Charlatans and scoundrels lurk in dark corners,
awaiting the unsuspecting. Don't be their prey.

*The Stonehenge Plus system TURNED $5,000 INTO $1,000,000
in JUST 5 YEARS. Stonehenge Plus was invented by Stupendus
Magnificus, a NASA scientist who discovered a way to use the same
process used to launch the Mars Rover for trading currencies.
OVER 90% ACCURATE, it hasn't had a losing month
in 10 years. It is so good we are only going to sell 100 COPIES.
Get yours now while there is still time for only $1,999.*
—Advertisement from a system vendor

Anyone who has been around trading for any amount of time
has seen ads like this one, as has anyone who has his or her
name on a mailing list and is interested in trading. But buyer
beware: There are charlatans who use irresponsible marketing tactics and unrealistic backtest results to tout their newest inventions.

Many of those vendors build systems that they know will never yield returns at the levels they are advertising. Many of them intentionally alter the tests to make their systems look better than they really are. However, not all vendors are that unscrupulous. There are some who sell systems that they believe will work well without realizing that their basic methods are flawed or knowing the limitations of historical testing and the pitfalls of using historical test results to predict future performance. Of course, there are those who are skilled at avoiding the pitfalls of historical testing. Unfortunately, these vendors are very few in number and it is extremely difficult for an inexperienced trader to distinguish between the systems that have been developed using good testing methods and those that have not.

Even highly experienced traders often do not know the reasons why their systems perform much more poorly in actual trading than they do in historical simulations. They know this phenomenon exists and compensate for it but do not understand its causes. There are four major sources of the discrepancies traders often find between historical test results and what is encountered in actual trading:

- **Trader effects:** The fact that a particular method has made a lot of money in the recent past increases the likelihood that other traders will have noticed it and will start using similar ideas, increasing the chances that the method will not work as well as it did initially.

- **Random effects:** The historical test may have demonstrated better performance than the underlying edge normally would indicate as a result of purely random chance.

- **Optimization paradox:** The act of determining the particular parameter, such as choosing a 25-day moving average instead of a 30-day average, reduces the predictive value of the backtest itself.

- **Overfitting or curve fitting:** The system may be so complicated that it has no predictive value. Because it is tuned to the historical data so closely, a slight alteration in market behavior will produce markedly poorer results.

Trader Effects

An *observer effect* is a concept from physics in which the act of measuring a phenomenon sometimes affects that phenomenon; the observer disturbs the experiment by the act of observing. A similar thing happens in trading: The act of trading itself can change the underlying market conditions on which the success of a trade is predicated. I call this a *trader effect*. Anything that repeats with enough consistency is likely to be noticed by several market participants. Similarly, a strategy that has worked especially well in the recent past is likely to be noticed by many traders. However, if too many traders start to try to take advantage of a particular strategy, that strategy will cease working as well as it did previously.

Let us consider the breakout strategy. If you knew that there were going to be many large traders buying at the breakout in a relatively thin market, what could you do to make money from them? What strategy could you employ that would be like printing money?

You would buy your orders ahead of those of other traders and in so doing cause a rise in prices to the levels that triggered the orders from those large traders. Then you could sell your position back to them for a guaranteed profit; in effect you would have moved the price to take advantage of the other buyers.

Imagine that you are a gold trader. If you knew that there would be large buy orders from ACME, say, 1,000 contracts in August gold at $410.50, what might you be able to do?

If you could buy enough to reach those stops, you could make money by selling the contracts back when the stop was hit. On the one hand, if the price was far enough away from those stops, it might take more money than you had to guarantee that you could move the market to reach those buy orders. On the other hand, if the price was close enough, say, at $408.00, a series of buy market orders might raise the price enough to trigger those additional buy orders from ACME.

Since you would be buying and then quickly selling right afterward, you might change the meaning of a breakout itself. Before the addition of the trader effects, a breakout might have signified that resistance had been broken, and so there was a greater likelihood of favorable price movement when a breakout occurred. However, with the addition of the new buys, which are designed only to move the market enough to cause a breakout to occur, the meaning of the breakout has been altered.

Let us examine this concept using a specific example. Assume that there were no buyers willing to buy at $408.00 or higher but there were sellers willing to sell 1,000 contracts at anything above $409.00, and these sell orders would act as a ceiling keeping the price from going over $409.00. Before the addition of your buy orders, the market would not have advanced to the price of $410.50, and so the breakout would not have happened. Therefore, in a simulation for a breakout-based system that looked at this trade there would not have been a breakout and thus no trade.

Now suppose that in the same circumstances you enter the market and buy up those 1,000 contracts at an average price of $409.00; there are no more sellers at that price, and so you have to buy another 100 from the sellers at $411.00. This trade causes the large buyer to begin buying, at which time you sell him the 1,000 contracts at $411.00. Although he thinks he got a good price, you made an excellent trade. All that remains is to get rid of the extra 100 contracts. Since there are no buyers at the recent prices, you have to sell lower, and so you sell your 100 contracts back where the market had been trading: at $407.00. You lose $4 × 100 ounces on 100 contracts, or $40,000, but you made $2 × 100 ounces on 1,000 contracts for a new profit of $160,000 not counting commissions. Not bad for a few seconds' work.

What happened to those traders from ACME who had been counting on the edge in the breakout? They are sitting on a large position that was entered for reasons different from those their backtest would have indicated. This is the result of a trader effect.

One specific example of this is provided by a system that became very popular a few years back because it had maintained excellent performance for many years. For that reason, lots of brokers started to offer it to their customers. At one time I heard estimates that several hundred million dollars in aggregate was being traded using this system. Shortly after the system reached its peak in popularity, those trading it experienced a prolonged drawdown that was much longer and higher than anything that had occurred in 20 years of backtesting. The system had an exploitable flaw. If the closing price passed a certain level, there would be buy or sell orders on the following morning's open. Since other traders knew the price levels that would trigger those orders, it was a simple matter to buy on the close ahead of the next morning's open. One then could exit the position by selling just after the following day's open, which would generally be much higher because of all the buy orders that had been generated overnight as a result of the system's rules.

To make matters worse, the system's authors used portfolios that included illiquid markets such as lumber and propane, which could move quite a bit on relatively light volume, and so many people who traded with the system also traded those illiquid markets. I'm sure that one of the reasons for that system's sudden unprecedented drawdown was exactly this sort of anticipatory buying, which effectively ruined its edge for a time. Other traders are not that dense. They will exploit any repeated patterns that they notice. This is one of the reasons why it is better to develop your own system; you can build a system with which it is much less likely that you will have your edge ruined by trader effects because other traders will not know exactly when you will be buying or selling.

When we traded for Rich, there were often times when we would all be entering trades at essentially the same time. Market traders knew that when they started to get large orders from us, the orders probably would continue for quite some time. For that reason, at times the floor traders and brokers would start to move the market ahead of our orders. Since we used limit orders, this was a bit more risky—that was one of the reasons we used limit orders—because we would not get filled in those circumstances and so we could pull our orders. Sometimes when I wanted to buy and knew that the market was particularly prone to having the locals move it in antic-ipation of our orders, I would send fake orders in the opposite direction. Then, if the market moved, I would cancel the original order and place a limit order much closer to the market or even on the other side of the ask. For example, if I wanted to buy 100 contracts, I might first place a fake sell order. If that fake order was a sell of 100 contracts at $415 and the market was trading at $410 bid and $412 ask, the presence of the order might move the market to $405 bid and $408 ask. I then might cancel the fake limit order and enter one to buy at a $410 limit that probably would get filled at $408 or $410, which was the original ask before my first order.

I did not do this very often, just enough to keep other traders guessing about what we were doing. In some respects it was a bit like bluffing in poker. You cannot bluff all the time or you'll get called and end up losing the bluffs and your bets. However, an occasional bluff can help your play considerably because it forces the other players to call you sometimes when you actually have a good hand, resulting in a larger pot when you have the winning hand. You also may win pots with the bluff, and that also increases your winnings.

Just as an occasional bluff makes it harder for your opponents to figure out what you are doing, the Turtles added quite a bit of confusion for anyone who was trying to figure out how Richard Dennis was trading. Some of us used small stops, some used larger ones, some of us bought right at the breakout, some just after, some just before; in all we created a lot of obfuscation that probably helped him get better fills for his orders.

Note that a trader effect can occur without any conscious attempt by traders to front-run other traders' orders. If too many traders attempt to exploit a given market phenomenon, that can ruin the edge for that phenomenon, at least for a period, because their orders will tend to dilute the edge. This problem is especially prevalent in arbitrage-type trading, where the edge is relatively small.

Random Effects

Most traders do not understand the degree to which completely random chance can affect their trading results. The typical investor understands this even less than the typical trader does. Even very experienced investors such as those who operate and make decisions for pension funds and hedge funds generally do not understand the extent of this effect. Results can vary to an amazing degree solely on the basis of random events. The amount of variation displayed in a series of historical simulations that include random events is surprisingly high. This section examines the range of possibilities that could be due entirely to random effects in the domain of long-term trend following.

In the discussion of the edge ratio I ran a simulation for an entry that randomly enters long or short at the open, depending on the computer equivalent of a coin flip. I created a complete system that combines random entries based on a coin flip with a time-based exit some number of days later within the range of 20 days to 120 days. I then ran 100 tests with the same data that was used in Chapter 10 to compare trend-following strategies. The best test in the simulation returned 16.9 percent and turned $1 million into about $5.5 million in the 10.5 years of the test. The worst test in the simulation lost 20 percent per year. This shows that there is a good deal of variance that is due entirely to random events.

What happens if we add a little edge? What if we make our system similar to a trend-following system by including the trend filter we use with the Donchian Trend system so that trades are entered randomly, but only if they are in the same direction as the major trend? The answers to these questions are interesting because if you examine the track record of any group of trend-following funds, there is a lot of variance in performance. If the performance of a particular fund is good, the manager of that fund will say, of course, that this success is due to superior strategies and execution. Superior performance actually may be due to random effects rather than superior strategies. You can understand this better if you consider the extent to which those random effects can influence outcomes when there is some edge.

If you add a trend filter with a positive edge to the completely random system, the average performance for 100 tests moves up considerably. In my simulation, the average return rose to 32.46 percent and the average drawdown dropped to 43.74 percent. Even with the addition of the trend filter, there remains a large variance among the individual tests. Out of 100 random tests in the simulation, the single best test showed returns of 53.3 percent, a MAR ratio of 1.58, and a maximum drawdown of 33.6 percent. The worst test showed returns of 17.5 percent with a drawdown of 62.7 percent.

Luck or random effects play a large role in the performance of actual traders and actual funds even though the best traders do not like to admit that to their investors. Investors believe that a track record is more definitive than it actually is. For example, anyone investing in a particular fund generally expects to achieve performance after investment similar to the fund's historical performance. The problem is that it is impossible to know the difference between a truly great trading operation that is having average luck and an average trading operation that is having excellent luck if one looks only at the track record. The random effects are too large and common for that to be known with certainty.

Consider the best track record from the 100-test simulation that was cited above. If one traded less aggressively, for example, at 25 percent of the level we did as Turtles, one of the tests would have achieved returns of 25.7 percent with a drawdown of 17.7 percent with a 10-year track record. We all know that a trader who entered randomly would not be more likely in the future to perform at the same level since there is no edge in trading randomly. Unfortunately, for anyone looking only at a track record, out of a large group of traders some will have been lucky enough to seem to know what they are doing when they actually do not.

Lucky Genes

Another way to understand random effects is to look at their existence in nature. Intelligence, height, athletic ability, singing ability—all these qualities are the result of random effects. If you have good genes for a particular trait (i.e., your parents both had a particular trait), you are much more likely than most people to have that trait, though perhaps not to the same degree. If your father and mother are both very tall, you probably will be very tall, but the farther they drift from the norm, the more likely you are to be shorter than they are.

In genetics and in statistics this is known as *reversion to the mean* or *the regression effect*. A person with very tall parents also has parents with tall genes and a very lucky combination of those genes from a height perspective. But a person with lucky genes is able to pass on his genes but not his luck, and so a child born to those parents is more likely to be closer to average since that child is not as likely to have the same "lucky" arrangement of the genes that the parents did.

Bad News for Investors

When one starts to use performance measures to separate a group of funds into the good ones and the underperforming ones, one is very likely to encounter random effects. The reason for this is that there are more lucky average traders than unlucky good traders. Consider a universe of 1,000 traders in which perhaps 5 or 6 are truly excellent traders. If 80 percent of the 1,000 are close to average traders, there are only 5 or 6 traders who have an opportunity to get unlucky, but there are 800 with the opportunity to get lucky. If 2 percent of traders get lucky enough to have a good track record for 10 years—and the test described above shows that the actual number is probably even higher than that—this means that there is a group of 21 traders with excellent performance, only one-quarter of whom are actually excellent traders.

Luck and Time

Time tends to favor the truly excellent traders rather than merely the lucky ones. If there are 16 traders who are lucky for 10 years, after another 15 years their performance is much more likely to be closer to average. Conversely, if you consider only 5-year track records, the number of seemingly excellent traders who are actually only lucky traders skyrockets. This is because over shorter measurement periods the extent of the random effects is also much greater.

What happens to variance in our test if we use a shorter time frame, perhaps only the 3.5 years from January 2003 through June 2006? For this period, the average performance for the random entry system was a 35 percent return with a MAR ratio of 1.06. The real systems did considerably better. The Triple Moving Average system returned 48.5 percent with a MAR ratio of 1.50. The Bollinger Breakout system returned 52.2 percent with a MAR ratio of 1.54. The Dual Moving Average system returned 49.7 percent with a MAR ratio of 1.25.

As for the random tests, how many lucky traders emerged from the 100 tests in the simulation? How many beat our best system's performance purely on the basis of luck? Seventeen out of 100 had a MAR ratio better than 1.54; of those 17 tests, 7 had a return higher than 52.2 percent. The very best random trader returned 71.4 percent with a drawdown of 34.5 percent for a MAR ratio of 2.07. All this is something to think about the next time you are looking at a three-year track record with excellent performance.

When you are looking at a short-term track record, you should realize that much of what you are seeing is attributable to luck. If you want to know whether a particular trader is one of the lucky average or one of the excellent few, you need to dig deeper than the track record and focus on the people behind the track record.

Good investors invest in people, not historical performance. They know how to identify traits that will lead to excellent performance in the future, and they know how to identify traits that are indicative of average trading ability. This is the best way to overcome random effects. The good news for those who are doing historical simulations is that it is fairly easy to detect when backtest results probably are due to random effects rather than to a system's edge. Chapter 12 will discuss ways in which this can be done, but first let's look at two more reasons why backtest results do not match reality.

Optimization

An effect that I call the optimization paradox is another reason for the divergence between tested results and actual results. This paradox is the cause of much confusion, especially for traders who are new to computer simulation. Optimization is the process of determining which particular numeric values to use in trading with a system that requires computations that employ specific numbers. These numbers are called *parameters*. For example, the number of days in a long moving average is a parameter; the number of days in a short moving average is another parameter. Optimization is the process of choosing the best, or optimum, values for those parameters. Many traders say that optimization is bad because it leads to curve fitting and results in poor performance. I say that's bunk!

Optimization is good when it is done correctly because it is always better to understand the performance characteristics of changes to a parameter than to be ignorant of them. An examination of the changes in the performance measures of a parameter often reveals signs that performance is due to random effects or overfitting rather than to the edge of a system. Optimization is simply the process of discovering the impact on the results of varying a particular parameter across different values and then using that information to make an informed decision about which specific parameter value to use in actual trading.

Traders who believe that optimization is bad or dangerous think that way because they do not understand the optimization paradox and because they have seen the effects of improper optimization that leads to what is known in statistics as *overfitting*.

The Optimization Paradox

The optimization paradox states that parameter optimization results in a system that is *more likely* to perform well in the future but *less likely* to perform as well as the simulation indicates. Thus, optimization improves the likely performance of the system while decreasing the predictive accuracy of the historical simulation metrics. I believe that an incomplete understanding of this paradox and its causes has led many traders to shy away from optimizing systems out of a fear of overoptimizing or curve fitting a system. However, I contend that proper optimization is always desirable.

Using parameter values that result from proper optimization should increase the likelihood of getting good results in actual trading in the future. A specific example will help explain this. Consider the Bollinger Breakout system, which has two parameters. Figure 11-1 shows a graph of the values for the MAR ratio as the entry threshold parameter, which defines the width of the volatility channel in standard deviation, varies from 1 standard deviation to 4 standard deviations.

Note how the results for a channel with a width of 2.4 standard deviations are the peak for this simulation. Any value for the entry threshold that is less than 2.4 or greater than 2.4 results in a test that shows a lower MAR ratio.

Now, returning to our premise that optimization is beneficial, suppose we had not considered optimizing the channel width and instead had decided arbitrarily to use a channel width of 3.0 since we recalled from high-school statistics that 99-plus percent of values for normal distributions fall within 3 standard deviations of the average. If the future is fairly close to the past, we would have been leaving a lot of money on the table and would have subjected our

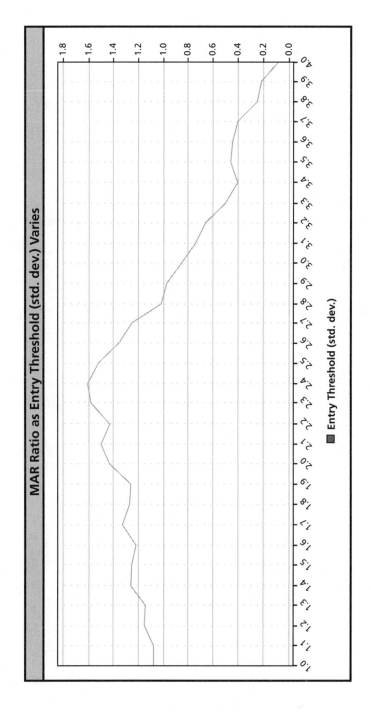

Figure 11-1 Change in MAR Ratio as the Entry Threshold Varies

trading to much greater drawdowns than a 2.4-standard deviation entry threshold would have provided. To give you an idea how great that difference could have been, consider that the test at 2.4 makes 8 times as much money over the 10.5-year test with the same drawdown as the test at 3.0 does, with returns of 54.5 percent versus 28.2 percent for the test with an entry threshold of 3.0.

Not optimizing means leaving things to chance through ignorance. Having seen the effects of changes to this parameter, we now have a much greater understanding of the performance ramifications of the entry threshold parameter and how the results are sensitive to that parameter. We know that if the channel width is too narrow, you get too many trades, and that hurts performance; if it is too wide, you have given up too much of the trend while waiting to enter, and that also hurts performance. Not doing this research because you were afraid of over optimizing or curve fitting would have deprived you of a good deal of useful knowledge that could materially improve your trading results and give you other ideas for better systems in the future. The following sections introduce you to a few more parameters, which you can see also have a mountain or hill shape when they are varied.

Moving Average Days Parameter

Figure 11-2 shows a graph of the values for the MAR ratio as the number of days in the moving average, which defines the center of the Bollinger band volatility channel, varies from 150 to 500.

Note how the results for the 350-day value are the peak for this test. Any value that is less than 350 or greater than 350 results in a test with a lower MAR ratio.

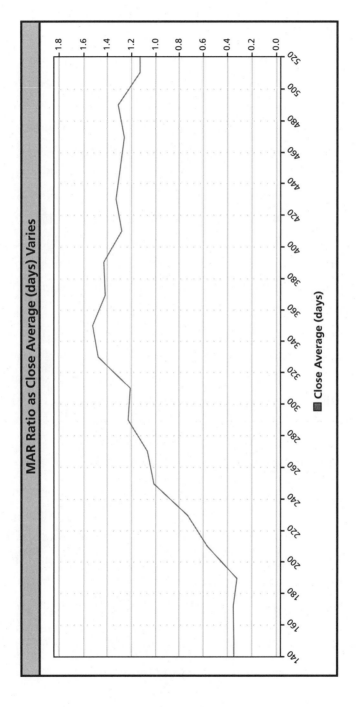

Figure 11-2 Change in MAR Ratio as the Number of Days in the Moving Average Varies

Figure 11-1 showed a graph of the values for the MAR ratio as the exit threshold parameter varies. The exit threshold is a parameter that defines the point of exit. In the book's earlier discussion of the Bollinger Breakout system, the system exited when the close crossed the moving average that defined the center of the channel. In this test I wanted to see what would happen if the system exited either before or after the crossover. For long trades a positive exit threshold means the number of standard deviations above the moving average, and for short trades it means the number of standard deviations below it. Negative values mean below the moving average for long trades and above the moving average for short trades. A value of zero for this parameter is the same as the original system, which exited at the moving average.

Consider what happens as the exit threshold varies from –1.5 to 1.0, as shown in Figure 11-3. Notice how the results for the –0.8 value are the peak for this test. Any value that is less than –0.8 or greater than –0.8 results in a test that shows a lower MAR ratio.

The Basis of Predictive Value

A historical test has predictive value to the extent that it shows performance that a trader is likely to encounter in the future. The more the future is like the past, the more future trading results will be similar to the results of historical simulation. A big problem with using historical testing as a means of system analysis is that the future will never be exactly like the past. To the extent that a system captures its profits from the effects of unchanging human behavioral characteristics that are reflected in the market, the past offers a reasonable approximation of the future, though never an

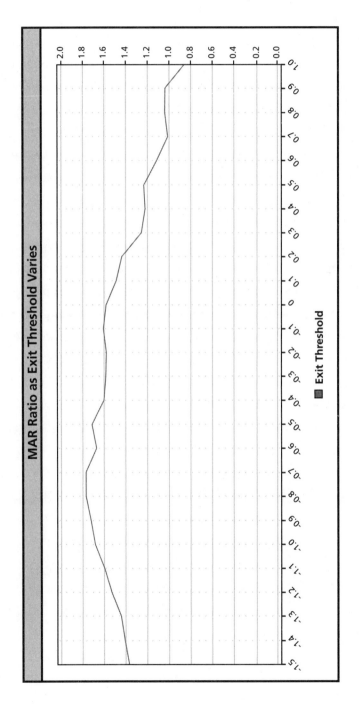

Figure 11-3 Change in MAR Ratio as the Exit Threshold Varies

exact one. The historical results of a test run with all optimized parameters represent a very specific set of trades: those trades which would have resulted if the system had been traded with the very best parameters. The corresponding simulation results represent a best-case view of the past.

One should expect to get these results in actual trading if the future corresponds *exactly* to the past, but that will never happen! Now consider the graphs displayed in the figures throughout this chapter: Each graph has a shape like the top of a mountain with a peak value. One might represent a given parameter with the graph shown in Figure 11-4.

If the value at point A represents a typical nonoptimized parameter value and the value at point B represents an optimized parameter, I argue that B represents a *better parameter value to trade* but one where the future actual trading results *probably will be worse* than that indicated by historical tests.

Parameter A is the *worse parameter to trade* but the one with *better predictive value* because if the system is traded at that value,

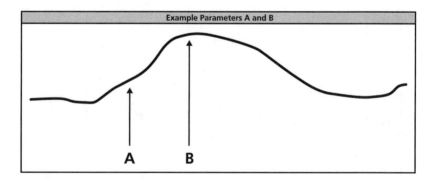

Figure 11-4 Example Parameters A and B

future actual results are just as likely to be better than or worse than those indicated by the historical tests that use value A for the parameter.

Why is this? To make it clearer, let's assume that the future will vary in such a way that it is likely to alter the graph slightly to the left or the right, but we do not know which. The graph in Figure 11-5 shows A and B with a band of values to the left and right that represent the possible shifts that result from the future being different from the past that we'll call margins of error.

In the case of value A, any shifts of the optimal parameter value to the left of A on the graph will result in *worse* performance than point A, and any shifts of the optimal parameter value right of A will result in *better* performance. Thus, the test result with a parameter value of A represents a decent predictor regardless of how the future changes since it is just as likely to be underpredicting as overpredicting the future.

This is not the case with value B. In all cases, any shift at all, either to the left or to the right, will result in worse performance.

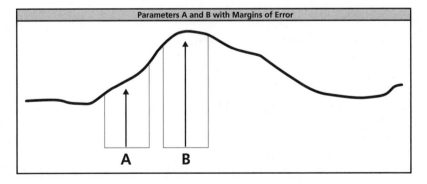

Figure 11-5   Parameters A and B with Margins of Error

This means that a test run with a value of B is very likely to over-predict the future results. When this effect is compounded across many different parameters, the effect of a drift in the future also will be compounded. This means that with many optimized parameters it becomes more and more unlikely that the future will be as bright as the predictions of the testing done with those optimized parameters.

This *does not mean* that we should use value A in our trading. Even in the event of a sizable shift, the values around the B point are *still higher* than those around the A point. Thus, even though optimization reduces the predictive value, you still want to trade using values that are likely to give good results in the event of drift.

The optimization paradox has been the source of much deception and scamming. Many unscrupulous system vendors have used the very high returns and incredible results made possible through optimization, especially over shorter periods, by using market-specific optimization to show historical results that they know cannot be achieved in actual trading. However, the fact that optimization can result in tests that overstate likely future results does not mean that optimization should not be performed. Indeed, optimization is critical to the building of robust trading systems.

Overfitting or Curve Fitting

Scammers also use other methods to generate historical results that are unrealistic. The most unscrupulous ones intentionally overfit or curve fit their systems. Overfitting often is confused with the optimization paradox, but they concern different issues.

Overfitting occurs when systems become too complex. It is possible to add rules to a system that will improve its historical performance, but that happens only because those rules affect a very small number of important trades. Adding those rules can create overfitting. This is especially true for trades that occur during critical periods in the equity curve for the system. For example, a rule that lets you exit a particularly large winning trade close to the peak certainly would improve performance but would be overfit if it did not apply to enough other situations.

I have seen many examples where system vendors have used this technique to improve results of their systems after a period of relatively poor performance. They sometimes sell the new improved systems as *plus* or *II* versions of their original systems. Anyone contemplating a purchase of a system "improved" in this matter would do well to investigate the nature of the rules which constitute the improvements to make sure that they have not benefited from overfitting.

I often find it useful to look at examples of a phenomenon taken to the extreme to understand it better. Here I will present a system that does some pretty egregious things that overfit the data. We will start with a very simple system, the Dual Moving Average system, and add rules that start to overfit the data.

Remember that this system had a very nasty drawdown in the last six months. Therefore, I will add a few new rules to fix that drawdown and improve performance. I am going to reduce my positions by a certain percentage when the drawdown reaches a particular threshold and then, when the drawdown is over, resume trading at the normal size.

To implement this idea, let's add a new rule to the system with two new parameters for optimization: the amount to be reduced and the threshold at which that reduction occurs. Looking at our simulation's equity curve, I decide that reducing positions by 90 percent when I reach a drawdown of 38 percent will limit the drawdowns. The addition of this rule improves the returns, which go from 41.4 percent without the rule to 45.7 percent with it, and the drawdown drops from 56.0 percent to 39.2 percent, with the MAR ratio going from 0.74 to 1.17. One might think, "This is a great rule; the system is now much better." However, this is completely incorrect!

The problem is that there is only *one time during the entire test* when this rule comes into play. It happens at the very end of the test, and I've taken advantage of my knowledge of the equity curve to construct the rules, and so the system has been fitted intentionally to the data. "What's the harm?" you ask. Consider the shape of the graph in Figure 11-6, where we vary the threshold for the drawdown where a reduction kicks in.

You may notice the rather abrupt drop in performance if we use a drawdown threshold of less than 37 percent. In fact, a 1 percent change in the drawdown threshold makes the difference between earning 45.7 percent and losing 0.4 percent per year. The reason for the drop in performance is that there is an instance in August 1996 where this rule kicks in and we cut back the position size so much that the system does not earn enough money to dig out of the hole created by the drawdown. Perhaps this is not such a good rule. It worked in the first instance only because the drawdown was so close to the end of the test.

Traders call this phenomenon a *cliff*. The presence of cliffs—large changes in results for a very small change in parameter values—is a good indication that you have overfit the data and can expect results in actual trading that are wildly different from those

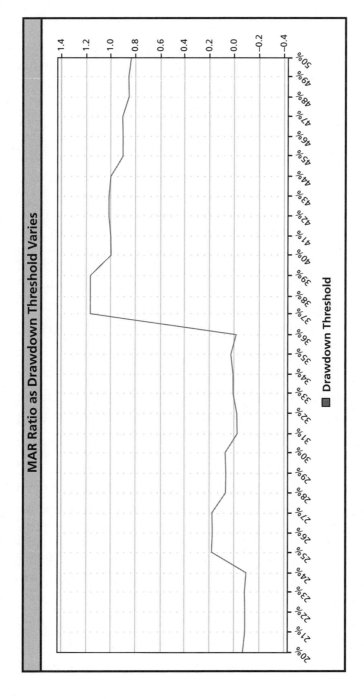

Figure 11-6 Change in MAR Ratio as the Number of Days in the Moving Average Varies

which you achieved in testing. It is also another reason why optimizing parameters is good: You can see cliffs and fix the source of the problem before you start trading.

The Importance of Sample Size

As was noted briefly in Chapter 2, people tend to place too much importance on a small number of instances of a particular phenomenon despite the fact that from a statistical perspective very little information can be drawn from a few instances of any event. This is the primary cause of overfitting. Rules that do not come into play very often can cause inadvertent overfitting, which leads to a divergence in performance between backtests and real trading.

This can happen inadvertently over the course of many instances because most people are not used to thinking in these terms. A good example is seasonality. If one tests for seasonal changes in 10 years of data, there will be at most 10 instances of a particular seasonal phenomenon since there are only 10 years of data. There is very little statistical value in a sample size of 10, and so any tests using those data will not be good predictors of future performance.

Let's consider a rule that ignores this concept and uses the computer to help us find the perfect way to overfit to our data. You might notice that September was a bad month for a few years; then you might test a rule that lightens positions in September by a certain percentage. Since you have a computer, you might decide to have it search for any sort of seasonally bad periods in which you should lighten up.

I did this for the system in this chapter. Then I ran 4,000 tests that tested reducing positions at the beginning of each month and then lightening up by a certain percentage for a certain number of days and then resuming the previous position size when that number of days had passed. I found two such periods in the 10 years of data I used for testing. If one lightens up 96 percent for the first 2 days of September and the first 25 days of July, one can get better results. How much better?

The addition of this rule improves our returns, which move from 45.7 percent without the rule to 58.2 percent with it, and our drawdown goes up a tiny bit from 39.2 percent to 39.4 percent, whereas the MAR ratio goes from 1.17 to 1.48. Again we think: "This is a great rule; my system is now much better."

Unfortunately, this rule works only because there were significant drawdowns during those periods in the past, not because there is something magical about those periods. It is not very likely that the drawdowns will occur on the same dates in the future. This is an example of the worst kind of overfitting, but you would be surprised how many otherwise intelligent people fall prey to this sort of trap.

If you do not know this, you might think that the system is good enough to start trading with it. You might even start to raise money from friends and family by telling them about this wonderful system and its results. The problem is that you really have a system that returned 41.4 percent, not 58.2 percent; a drawdown of 56.0 percent, not 39.4 percent; and a MAR ratio of 0.74, not 1.48. You are bound to be disappointed with the real performance because you have been seduced by the easy improvements of curve fitting.

Next I'll examine ways to avoid the problems discussed in this chapter. I'll show ways to determine what you actually may be able to achieve from a system in order to minimize the impact of trader effects, detect random effects, properly optimize, and avoid overfitting to the historical data.

twelve

ON SOLID GROUND

Trading with poor methods is like learning to juggle while standing in a rowboat during a storm. Sure, it can be done, but it is much easier to juggle when one is standing on solid ground.

N ow that you are aware of some of the major ways in which you can get inaccurate results from backtests, you may be wondering: "How can I determine what I might actually be able to achieve?" or "How do I avoid the problems described in Chapter 11?" or "How do I test the right way?" This chapter will discuss the general principles of doing proper backtesting. A thorough understanding of the underlying causes of the backtesting predictive errors discussed in Chapter 11 is an important prerequisite for this chapter, and so it is a good idea to reread that chapter carefully if you only skimmed it the first time.

At best, you can get a rough sense of what the future holds by looking at the results of historical simulation. However, fortunately, even a rough idea can provide enough edge to enable a good trader to make a lot of money. To understand the factors that affect the margin of error, or *degree of roughness*, for your ideas, you need to look at a few basic statistical concepts that provide the basis for historical testing. Since I am not a big fan of books filled with formulas and lengthy explanations, I will try to keep the math light and the explanations clear.

Statistical Basis for Testing

Proper testing takes into account the statistical concepts that affect the descriptive ability of the tests as well as the limitations inherent in those descriptions. Improper testing can make you overconfident when in reality there is little or no assurance the test results have any predictive value. In fact, bad tests may provide the wrong answer entirely.

Chapter 11 covered most of the reasons why historical simulations are at best rough estimates of the future. This chapter shows how to increase the predictive ability of testing and get the best rough estimate possible.

The area of statistics relating to inference by sampling from a population is also the basis for the predictive potential of testing through the use of historical data. The basic idea is that if you have a sufficiently large sample, you can use measurements made on that sample to infer likely ranges of measurements for the entire group. So, if you look at a sufficiently large sample of past trades for a particular strategy, you can draw conclusions about the likely future performance of that strategy. This is the same area of statistics that pollsters use to make inferences about the behavior of a larger population. For example, after polling 500 people drawn randomly from every state, pollsters draw conclusions about all the voters in the United States. Similarly, scientists assess the effectiveness of a particular drug for the treatment of a particular disease on the basis of a relatively small study group because there is a statistical basis for that inference.

The two major factors that affect the statistical validity of the inferences derived from a sample of a population are the size of the sample and the degree to which the sample is representative of the overall population. Many traders and new system testers understand sample size at a conceptual level but believe that it refers only to the number of trades in a test. They do not understand that the statistical validity of tests can be lessened even when they cover thousands of trades if *particular rules or concepts apply to only a few instances* of those trades.

They also often ignore the necessity that a *sample be representative of the larger population* as this is messy and hard to measure without some subjective analysis. A system tester's underlying assumption is that the past is representative of what the future is likely to bring. If this is the case and there is a sufficiently large sample, we can draw inferences from the past and apply them to the future. If the sample is not representative of the future, the testing is not useful and will not tell us anything about the likely future performance of the system that is being tested. Thus, *this assumption is critical*. If a representative sample of 500 people is sufficient to determine who the new president is likely to be with a 2 percent margin of error using a *representative sample*, would polling 500 attendees at the Democratic National Convention tell us anything about the voting of the overall population? Of course it wouldn't because the sample would not be representative of the population —it only includes Democrats whereas the actual U.S. voting population includes many Republicans who were not included in the sample; Republicans probably will vote for candidates different from the ones your poll indicated. When you make a sampling mistake like this, you get *an* answer, perhaps even the one you want, but it is not necessarily the *right* answer.

Pollsters understand that *the degree to which a sample truly reflects the population it is intended to represent is the key issue.* Polls conducted with samples that are not representative are inaccurate, and pollsters get fired for conducting inaccurate polls. *In trading, this is also the key issue.* Unfortunately, unlike pollsters, who generally understand the statistics of sampling, most traders do not. This is perhaps most commonly seen when traders paper trade or backtest over only the very most recent history. This is like polling at the Democratic convention.

The problem with tests conducted over a short period is that during that period the market may have been in only one or two of the market states described in Chapter 2, perhaps only in a stable and volatile state, in which reversion to the mean and countertrend strategies work well. If the market changes its state, the methods being tested may not work as well. They may even cause a trader to lose money. So, testing must be done in a way that maximizes the likelihood that the trades taken in the test are representative of what the future may hold.

Existing Measures Are Not Robust

In testing, you are trying to determine relative performance, assess potential future performance, and determine whether a particular idea has merit. One of the problems with this process is that the generally accepted performance measures are not very stable—they are not robust. This makes it difficult to assess the relative merits of an idea because small changes in a few trades can have a large effect on the values of these nonrobust measures. The effect of the instability in the measures is that it can cause one to believe that an idea has more merit than it actually has or discard an idea because it does not appear to have as much promise as it might when examined using more stable measures.

A statistic is robust if changing a small part of the data set does not change that statistic significantly. The existing measures are too sensitive to changes in the data, too jumpy. This is one of the reasons that in doing historical simulation for trading system research, slight differences in parameter values cause relatively large differences in some of the measures; the measures themselves are not robust (i.e., they are too sensitive to small portions of the data). Anything that affects those small portions can affect the results too greatly. This makes it easy to overfit and to fool yourself with results that you will not be able to match in real life. The first step in testing the Turtle Way is to address this issue by finding performance measures that are robust and not sensitive to small changes in the underlying data.

One of the questions that Bill Eckhardt asked me during my initial interview for the Turtle position was: "Do you know what a robust statistical estimator is?" I stared blankly for a few seconds and admitted: "I have no idea." (I now can answer that question. There is a branch of mathematics that tries to address the issue of imperfect information and poor assumptions; it is called *robust statistics*.)

It is clear from the question that Bill had respect for the imperfect nature of testing and research based on historical data as well as knowledge of the unknown that was rare at that time and is still rare. I think this is one of the reasons Bill's trading performance has held up so well over the years.

This is yet another example of how far ahead of the industry Rich and Bill's research and thinking were. The more I learn, the deeper my respect for their contribution to the field becomes. I am also surprised at how little the industry has advanced beyond what Rich and Bill knew in 1983.

Robust Performance Measures

Earlier chapters in this book used the MAR ratio, CAGR%, and the Sharpe ratio as comparative performance measures. These measures are not robust, since they are very sensitive to the start and end dates for a test. This is especially true for tests of less than 10 years. Consider what happens when we adjust the start and end dates for a test by a few months. To illustrate this effect, let's run a test that starts on February 1, 1996, instead of January 1 and that ends on April 30 instead of June 30, 2006, removing just one month from the beginning of the test and two months from the end.

A test of the Triple Moving Average system with the original test dates returns 43.2 percent with a MAR ratio of 1.39 and a Sharpe ratio of 1.25. With the revised start and stop dates, the return jumps to 46.2 percent, with the MAR ratio increasing to 1.61 and the Sharpe ratio increasing to 1.37. A test of the ATR Channel Breakout system with the original dates shows returns of 51.7 percent, a MAR ratio of 1.31, and a Sharpe ratio of 1.39. With the revised dates, the return climbs to 54.9 percent, the MAR ratio increases to 1.49, and the Sharpe ratio increases to 1.47.

The reason we see this sensitivity across all three measures is that the MAR ratio and the Sharpe ratio have return as a component of their numerators and return, whether expressed by CAGR% used for MAR or monthly average return used for the Sharpe ratio, is sensitive to start and stop dates. The maximum drawdown can also be sensitive to start and stop dates when that drawdown occurs near the beginning or end of a test. This has the effect of making the MAR ratio especially sensitive since it is composed of two components, both of which are sensitive to start and end dates; therefore, the effect of a change gets multiplied during the computation of this ratio.

The reason CAGR% is sensitive to changes in start and stop dates is that it represents the slope of the smooth line that goes from the start of the test to the end of the test on a logarithmic graph; changing the start and stop dates can change the slope of that line significantly. Figure 12-1 shows this effect.

Note how the slope of the line labeled "Revised Test Dates" is higher than that of the line labeled "Original Test Dates." In the example above there was a drawdown at the beginning of the test

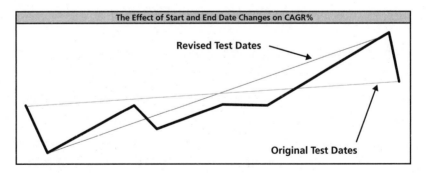

Figure 12-1 The Effect of Changes in the Start and End Dates on CAGR%

during January 1996; there was also a drawdown in the last two months of the test: May and June 2006. So, by moving the test dates a few months, we were able to eliminate both of those drawdowns. This is the same effect seen in Figure 12-1: Removing a drawdown on either end of a test will increase the slope of the line that defines CAGR%.

Regressed Annual Return (RAR%)

A better measure of the slope is a simple *linear regression* of all the points in each line. For readers who do not like math, a linear regression is a fancy name for what sometimes is called a *best fit line*. The best way to think about this is to realize that it represents the straight line that goes through the middle of all the points, much like what would happen if you stretched the graph and removed all the bumps by pulling on the ends without changing the overall direction of the graph.

This linear regression line and the return it represents create a new measure that I call the *regressed annual return*, or RAR% for short. This measure is much less sensitive to changes in the data at the end of the test. Figure 12-2 shows how the slope of the line changes much less when the endpoints for RAR% change.

We can see how the RAR% measure is less sensitive to changes in the test dates by running the same comparison we ran earlier because the two lines are much closer to having the same slope. The RAR% for the original test is 54.67 percent, whereas the RAR% for the altered dates is 54.78 percent, only 0.11 percent higher. Contrast this with the CAGR% measure, which changed by 3.0 percent points from 43.2 percent to 46.2 percent. For this test, the

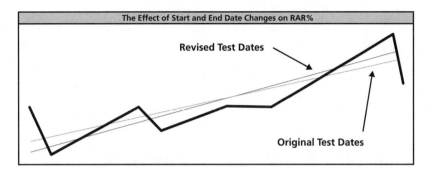

Figure 12-2   The Effect of Changes in the Start and End Dates on RAR%

CAGR% was almost 30 times more sensitive to the change in the end dates.

The monthly average return used in the Sharpe ratio is also sensitive to these changes because we are removing three bad months from the end of the tests, and that affects the average return, although the average return is affected less than the CAGR%. A better measure to use in the numerator would be the RAR%.

As was noted earlier, the maximum drawdown component of the MAR ratio is also sensitive to changes in start and end dates. If the largest drawdown is on either end of the test, the performance measure MAR will be affected considerably. The maximum drawdown is a single point on an equity curve, and so you are missing out on some valuable additional data. A better measure is one that includes more drawdowns. A system that had five large drawdowns of 32 percent, 34 percent, 35 percent, 35 percent, and 36 percent would be harder to trade than would a system that had drawdowns of 20 percent, 25 percent, 26 percent, 29 percent, and 36 percent.

Further, the extent of the drawdown is only one dimension: All 30 percent drawdowns are not the same. I would not mind a drawdown that lasted only two months before recovering to new highs nearly as much as I would mind one that took two years to reach new highs. The recovery time or the length of the drawdown itself is also very important.

R-Cubed: A New Risk/Reward Measure

To take all these factors into account, I have created a new risk/reward measure that I call the robust risk/reward ratio (RRRR). I also like to call it R-cubed since I still have a bit of the nerdy engineer in me and tend to do these sorts of things. R-cubed uses RAR% in the numerator and a new measure I call the length-adjusted average maximum drawdown in the denominator. There are two components to this measure: the average maximum drawdown and the length adjustment.

The average maximum drawdown is computed by taking the five largest drawdowns and dividing by 5. The length adjustment is made by taking the average maximum drawdown length in days and dividing it by 365 and then multiplying that number by the average maximum drawdown. The average maximum drawdown length is computed by using the same algorithm, that is, taking the five longest drawdowns and dividing by 5. So, if the RAR% was 50 percent and the average maximum drawdown was 25 percent and the average maximum drawdown length was one year, or 365 days, you would have an R-cubed value of 2.0, which comes from 50 percent/(25 percent × 365/365). R-cubed is a risk/reward measure that accounts for risk from both a severity perspective and a duration perspective. It does this by using measures that are less sensitive to changes in the start and end dates. The measure is more robust than the MAR ratio; that is, it is less likely to change when minor changes are made in the test.

Robust Sharpe Ratio

The robust Sharpe ratio is RAR% divided by the annualized standard deviation of the monthly return. This measure is less sensitive to changes in the data set for the same reason that RAR% is less sensitive than CAGR%, as was outlined above. Table 12-1 shows how the robust measures are less sensitive to changes in the end dates of the test.

Table 12-1   Normal versus Robust Measures

Normal Measures	Test 01/96 to 06/06	Test 02/96 to 04/06	Δ%
CAGR%	51.7%	54.4%	5.2%
MAR ratio	1.31	1.47	12.2%
Sharpe ratio	1.39	1.46	5%

Robust Measures	Test 01/96 to 06/06	Test 02/96 to 04/06	Δ%
RAR%	54.7%	4.9%	0.4%
R-cubed	3.31	3.63	9.7%
R-Sharpe	1.58	1.6	1.3%

As is shown in Table 12-1, robust measures are less sensitive to change than are the existing measures. The R-cubed measure is sensitive to the addition or removal of large drawdowns but less sensitive than is the MAR ratio. The impact of a single drawdown is diluted by the averaging process used in the R-cubed measure. All the robust measures were much less affected by these changes in data than were their counterparts. If this test had not changed the maximum drawdown, the R-cubed measure would have shown the same 0.4 percent change that RAR% shows and the differences between the measures *would have been even more dramatic* as the MAR would have changed 5.2 percent (the same as the CAGR% that is its numerator) and the R-cubed measure would have changed 0.4 percent.

Another example of how robust measures hold up better can be seen in the same performance comparison of our six basic systems from Chapter 7. Recall how the performance dropped considerably when we included the five months from July to November 2006. Tables 12-2 and 12-3 show that robust measures held up much better over the relatively adverse conditions of the last several months. Table 12-2 shows the percentage changes in RAR% compared with the percentage change in CAGR% for these systems.

Table 12-2 Robustness of CAGR% versus RAR%

System	CAGR% 06/06	11/06	Δ%	RAR% 06/06	11/06	Δ%
ATR CBO	52.4%	48.7%	–7.0%	54.7%	55.0%	0.5%
Bollinger CBO	40.7%	36.7%	–9.8%	40.4%	40.7%	0.6%
Donchian Trend	27.2%	25.8%	–5.2%	28.0%	26.7%	–4.6%
Donchian Time	47.2%	4%	–0.4%	45.4%	44.8%	–1.4%
Dual Moving Average	50.3%	42.4%	–15.7%	55.0%	53.6%	–2.6%
Triple Moving Average	41.6%	36.0%	–13.5%	41.3%	40.8%	–1.2%
Average Δ			**–8.6%**			**–1.4%**

The RAR% changed less than a sixth as much as the CAGR% over this time period. This demonstrates that the RAR% measure is much more robust than CAGR%, meaning that it will be more stable over time during actual trading. The same holds true for the risk/reward measure *R*-cubed compared with its less robust cousin the MAR ratio. Table 12-3 lists the percentage changes in *R*-cubed compared with the percentage change in the MAR ratio for these systems.

Table 12-3   Robustness of *R*-Cubed versus the MAR Ratio

System	MAR Ratio 06/06	11/06	Δ%	R⁴ 06/06	11/06	Δ%
ATR CBO	1.35	1.25	–7.4%	3.72	3.67	–1.4%
Bollinger CBO	1.29	1.17	–9.3%	3.48	3.31	–4.9%
Donchian Trend	0.76	0.72	–5.3%	1.32	1.17	–11.4%
Donchian Time	1.17	1.17	–0.0%	2.15	2.09	–2.8%
Dual Moving Average	1.29	0.77	–40.3%	4.69	3.96	–15.6%
Triple Moving Average	1.32	0.86	–34.9%	3.27	2.87	–12.2%
Average Δ			**–16.2%**			**–8.0%**

The *R*-cubed measure changed about half as much as the MAR ratio did for the period indicated.

Robust measures are also less susceptible to the effect of luck than nonrobust measures are. For example, a trader who happened to be on vacation and avoided the largest drawdown for a particular type of trading would show a relatively higher MAR ratio compared with his peers; this would be shown with R-cubed, since that single event will not have as large an effect on the R-cubed measure. You are more likely to get good test results that come from lack rather than repeating market behavior which can be exploited by a trader when you are using nonrobust measures, and that is yet another reason to use those that are robust.

Using robust measures also helps you avoid overfitting because they are less likely to show large changes caused by small numbers of events. Consider the effect of the rules added to improve our Dual Moving Average system in the discussion on overfitting. The rule that was added to cut down the size of the drawdown improved CAGR% from 41.4 percent to 45.7 percent (10.3 percent) and the MAR ratio from 0.74 to 1.17 (60 percent). In contrast, the robust measure RAR% changes from 53.5 percent to 53.75, or only 0.4 percent; likewise, the robust risk/reward measure R-cubed changes from 3.29 to 3.86, only 17.3 percent. Robust measures are less likely to show major improvement from changes in a small number of trades. Therefore, since curve fitting generally benefits only a small number of trades, when you use robust measures, you are less likely to see major improvements in performance from curve fitting.

Let's consider a few other factors that affect the reliability of backtests for predicting system performance in the future.

Representative Samples

Two major factors determine how likely our sample trades and test results are to be representative of what the future may bring:

- **Number of markets:** Tests run with more markets are more likely to include markets in various states of volatility and trendiness.
- **Duration of test:** Tests run over longer periods will cover more market states and be more likely to contain sections of the past that are representative of the future.

I recommend testing all the data to which you have access. It is much cheaper to buy data than it is to pay for the losses associated with using a system that you thought worked only because you had not tested it over a sufficient number of markets or a sufficient number of years. Won't you feel inept when your system stops working the first time you encounter a market condition that has existed three or four times in the last 20 years but was not part of your test?

Young traders are particularly susceptible to this sort of mistake. They think that the conditions they have seen are representative of those markets in general. They often do not realize how markets go through phases and change over time, often returning to conditions that previously existed. In trading as in life, the young often fail to see the value in studying the history that occurred before they existed. Be young, but don't be foolish: Study history.

Remember how everyone was a day trader and a genius during the Internet boom? How many geniuses survived the collapse when their previously successful methods stopped working? If they had done some testing, they would have realized that their methods were dependent on the particular market conditions of that boom, and so they would have stopped using them when those conditions were no longer present. Or perhaps they would have employed robust methods that work well in all conditions.

Sample Size

The concept of sample size is simple: You need a large enough sample to make valid statistical inferences. The smaller the sample, the rougher the guess provided by those inferences; the larger the sample, the better the guess provided by those inferences. There is no magic number; there is only larger is better, smaller is worse. A sample size of less than 20 will produce a large degree of error. A sample size of more than 100 is much more likely to have predictive value. A sample size of several hundred is probably sufficient for most testing. There are specific formulas and methodologies that will give you specific answers to the question of how large a sample is required, but unfortunately, those formulas are not designed for the types of data encountered in trading, where we do not have a nice neat distribution of potential outcomes such as the distribution of women's height in Figure 4-3.

However, the real challenge does not lie in deciding exactly how many samples you need. The difficulty arises in assessing the inferences from past data when one is considering particular rules that do not come into effect very often. So, for these types of rules there is no way to get a large enough sample. Take the behavior of markets at the end of large price bubbles. You can come up with some specific rules for those market conditions and even test them, but you will not have a very large sample on which to base your decisions. In these cases we need to understand that the tests do not tell us anywhere near as much as they would if we had a much larger sample. The seasonal tendencies I outlined earlier are another area where this problem arises.

In testing a new rule for a system, you have to try to measure how many times that particular rule affected the results. If a rule made a difference only four times during the course of the test, you do not have a statistical basis for deciding whether that rule is helping. It is too easy for the effects you see to be random. One solution to this problem is to find ways to generalize the rule so that it comes into play more often; that will increase the sample size and therefore the statistical descriptive value of tests for that rule.

There are two common practices that compound the problem of small sample sizes: single-market optimization and the building of overly complex systems.

- **Single-market optimization:** Optimization methods that are performed separately for each market are much more difficult to test with a sufficient sample size because a single market offers much less trading opportunity.

- **Complex systems:** Complex systems have many rules, and it becomes very difficult at times to determine how many times a particular rule may have come into effect or the degree of that effect. Therefore, it is harder to be confident in the statistical descriptive value of tests that are run using a complex system.

For these reasons, I do not recommend optimizing for single markets and prefer simple ideas that have stronger statistical meaning.

Back to the Future

Perhaps one of the most interesting questions in this regard is: How can you determine what you actually may be able to achieve in real trading?

The answer to this question makes sense only when you understand the factors that affect performance loss, the need for robust measures, and the need for a sufficient number of representative samples. Once you have this, you can start to think about the likely effect of drift and change in the markets and how even excellent systems that have been built by experienced traders fluctuate in terms of their results. The reality is that you do not know and cannot predict how a system will perform. The best you can do is use tools that provide a sense of the range of potential values and the factors that affect those values.

Lucky Systems

If a system has performed particularly well in the recent past, it may have been a matter of luck or there may have been ideal market conditions for that system. Generally, systems that have done well tend to have difficult periods after those good periods. Do not expect to be able to repeat that lucky performance in the future. It may happen, but do not count on it. You are more likely to experience a period of suboptimal performance.

Parameter Scrambling

A very good exercise one should always perform before considering trading with any particular system is what I call *parameter scrambling*. Take a few system parameters and change them by a considerable amount, say, 20 to 25 percent of their value. Pick a point that is considerably down the side of the optimization curves shown in Figures 12-1 and 12-2. Now look at the results for this test. Using the Bollinger Breakout system, I decided to see what would happen when we moved from the optimal values of 350 days and –0.8 for the exit threshold to 250 days and 0.0 for the exit threshold. This decreased the RAR% from 59 percent to 58 percent and the R-cubed value from 3.67 to 2.18: A fairly dramatic change. This is just the sort of dramatic change one might expect to get when going from testing using historical data to actual trading in the market.

Rolling Optimization Windows

Using *rolling optimization windows* is another exercise that is more directly parallel to the experience of going from testing to real trading. To do this, pick a date perhaps 8 or 10 years in the past and then optimize with all the data before that point, using the same optimization methods you normally would use and making the same sorts of trade-offs you normally would make, pretending that you have data available only up to that point. When you have finished determining the *optimal* parameter values, run a simulation of those parameters using data for the two years after the years of the optimization. How did the performance for the subsequent several years hold up?

Continue this process with a date a few more years into the future (about six or eight years in the past). How does this compare with your original test and the first rolling window? How does it compare with the test using your original parameter values, the optimal values based on having all the data available? Repeat the process until you have reached the current time frame.

To illustrate this, I ran an optimization of the Bollinger Breakout system in which I varied each of the three parameters across a

Table 12-4 Rolling Optimization Window Test versus Actual RAR%

Period	MA	Entry	Exit	RAR% Test	RAR% Actual	Δ%	R⁴ Test	R⁴ Actual	Δ%
1989 to 1998	280	1.8	-0.8	55.0%	58.5%	6.3%	7.34	5.60	-23.7%
1991 to 2000	280	1.8	-0.5	58.5%	58.8%	0.6%	5.60	5.32	-5.0%
1993 to 2002	260	1.7	-0.7	58.5%	59.3%	1.4%	7.68	3.94	-5.0%
1995 to 2004	290	1.7	-0.6	63.9%	57.7%	-8.3%	5.53	3.90	-29.5%
1997 to 2006	290	1.7	-0.6	55.1%	N/A	N/A	3.90	N/A	N/A

broad range. I then picked the optimal setting on the basis of the optimal position, generally near the point where the maximum *R*-cubed value was achieved. I ran this optimization for five separate 10-year tests. Table12-4 shows the performance of the rolling optimization for the year after the period indicated.

As you can see from the table, performance varies greatly from the tested value for each rolling period. Further, the optimal values are different for each time period tested. This illustrates the imprecision of the testing process and the variability one will encounter in making the transition from testing to actual trading.

Monte Carlo Simulation

Monte Carlo simulation is one way to determine the robustness of a system and answer questions such as: "What if the past had been just slightly different?" and "What might the future bring?" You could think of it as a way to generate slightly different alternative universes by using the data from the series of events that represent the actual past price data.

The term *Monte Carlo simulation* refers to a general class of methods that use random numbers to investigate a particular phenomenon. It is most useful with phenomena that are impossible or difficult to describe with mathematical precision. The name *Monte Carlo* comes from the city in Monaco that is famous for gambling casinos since those casinos offer many games whose outcomes are determined by random events: roulette, craps, blackjack, and the like. The method was used during the Manhattan Project by the scientists who created the atomic bomb, and its name comes from that era.

Those scientists were trying to determine the fission characteristics of uranium so that they could determine how much uranium mass would be necessary to make an atomic bomb. Enriched uranium was incredibly expensive, and so they could not afford to be wrong in their assessment or they would waste months of time, not to mention money, if the bomb didn't explode because there was not enough uranium. Similarly, if they overestimated and ended up using more uranium than they needed, it would add months to the schedule for testing. Unfortunately, the complex interactions of uranium atoms inside a bomb were impossible to model accurately with the methods of that period and would have required computing resources that were unavailable until recent times.

To determine the amount of fissionable uranium required, they needed to know what percentage of the neutrons emitted by an atom splitting would result in another atom splitting. The famous physicist Richard Feynman had the insight that they could determine the characteristics of the interactions of particular single neutron by using a team of mathematicians and then could determine whether that neutron was absorbed by another nucleus or split another atom. Feynman realized that they could use random numbers to represent the various types of neutrons that would be emitted when an atom split. If that was done thousands of times, they would be able to look at an accurate distribution of the fission characteristics of uranium that would allow them to determine how much material would be needed. Feynman knew that although he could not predict the future because the process was too complex, he could take the parts of the problem he did understand and, using random numbers to simulate neutron properties, obtain the answer to the problem anyway. So, he could understand the nature of the fission characteristics of uranium without having to be able to predict *exactly* what each atom would do at each point.

Alternative Trading Universes

The markets are even more complex than nuclear fission reactions. Markets are composed of the actions of thousands of people who make decisions on the basis of their own history and brain chemistry, which are much less predictable than neutrons are. Fortunately, as Feynman did with uranium analysis, we can use random numbers to get a better feel for the potential characteristics of a trading system even though we cannot predict what the future will bring. We can examine a set of alternative trading universes that represent a potential way in which history might have unfolded if things had been slightly different.

There are two common ways to use Monte Carlo methods to generate these alternative trading universes:

- **Trade scrambling:** Randomly changing the order and start dates of the trades from an actual simulation and then using the percentage gain or loss from the trades to adjust equity by using the new scrambled trade order

- **Equity curve scrambling:** Building new equity curves by assembling random portions of the original equity curve

Of these two approaches, equity curve scrambling generates more realistic alternative equity curves because Monte Carlo simulation with random trade reordering tends to understate the possibility of drawdowns.

The periods of maximum drawdown invariably occur at the tail end of large trends or periods of positive equity increases. At those times, markets tend to correlate more highly than they normally do. This is true for futures and stocks. At the end of a large trend when it breaks down and reverses, it seems that everything moves against you at once; even markets that normally do not seem correlated become so on those volatile days when a large trend disintegrates.

Because trade scrambling removes the connection between trades and dates, it also removes the effect on the equity curve of many trades simultaneously reversing. This means that your drawdowns show up with less magnitude and frequency in Monte Carlo simulation than they will in real life. Take a look at the moves in gold and silver in the spring of 2006. If you happened to test a trend-following system that traded both of those markets, scrambling the trades would mean that your drawdowns for those two markets would happen at different times, effectively reducing the effect of each separate drawdown. In fact, this effect extended to a few other relatively unlikely markets, such as sugar; there was a significant period of drawdown in the sugar market during the 20-day period from mid-May to mid-June 2006, the same period in which gold and silver were declining. Thus, trade scrambling is inferior because it understates the drawdowns one is likely to encounter in trading long-term and medium-term systems.

Another example of this phenomenon is the one-day drawdown in the 1987 U.S. stock market crash. On they day of the large opening gap in eurodollars, many markets that normally were not correlated also gapped strongly against my positions.

Monte Carlo simulation using scrambling of trades tends to dilute those very real occurrences because it spreads the trades apart so that they no longer have adverse price movement on the same days.

Many software packages that implement Monte Carlo simulation offer a way to generate new curves by using equity curve scrambling. However, they do not take into account another important issue. I also have found through testing and experience that the periods of bad days at the end of large trends and the magnitude of those bad days are much worse than one would expect from random events. At those times of major drawdown, the equity curve for a trend-following system exhibits serial correlation or correlation of one day's net change with the preceding day's net changes. Put more simply, the bad days tend to cluster in a way that one would not expect to occur randomly.

Using the same recent example of the drawdown in gold, silver, and sugar in spring 2006, if one scrambled only daily net changes, the long streak of high-magnitude changes in equity from mid-May to mid-June would be lost as it would be very unlikely that those changes would come together if you randomly drew from a distribution or even from the actual equity curve.

To account for this in our simulation software, at Trading Blox we use equity curve net changes but allow for scrambling by using multiday chunks of the curve rather than just a single day's change. That way the simulated equity curve preserves the grouping of bad days that one encounters in actual trading. In my testing, I use 20-day chunks for equity curve scrambling and find that this preserves the autocorrelation of the equity curve and gives the resulting simulation better real-world predictive value.

Monte Carlo Reports

What can we do with the simulated alternative equity curves that are generated using Monte Carlo? We can use them to build distributions of the results for a specific measure to determine the range of possible values one would see if the future was like any of the alternative universes we created through the simulation. Figure 12-3 shows a distribution that was created by generating 2,000 simulated alternative universe equity curves, computing the RAR% for each of those curves, and then plotting the distribution of those curves on a graph.

The vertical line intersecting the curved line at the top of the graph shows the RAR% value that 90 percent of the 2,000 simulated equity curves exceeded. In this case, 90 percent of the 2,000 alternative universe curves showed more than 42 percent RAR%.

Graphs like this one are good because they help you realize that the future is unknown and will come from a set of possibilities. However, one should be very careful not to read too much into the specifics of reports like these. Remember that these numbers are taken from an equity curve that is dependent on past data and therefore suffers from all the potential pitfalls outlined in Chapter 11. A Monte Carlo simulation does not make a poor test better since the simulated alternative universe equity curves are only as good as the historical simulation from which they are derived. If your RAR% is overstated by 20 percent because of the effect of the optimization paradox, a Monte Carlo simulation using the same optimized parameter values still will overstate the RAR% for the alternative universe equity curves generated in the simulation.

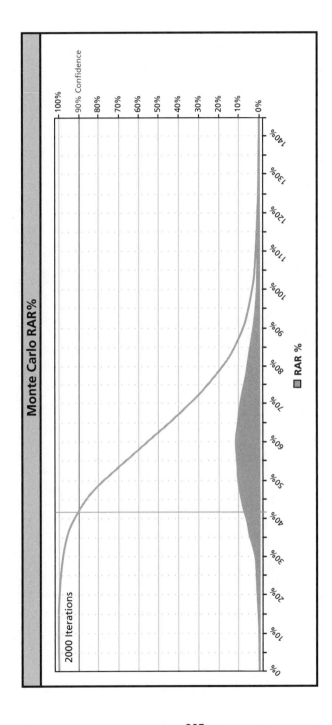

Figure 12-3 Monte Carlo Distribution of RAR%

Some Like It Rough

As the exercises above have demonstrated, a backtest is at best a rough approximation of what one may expect in the future. Robust measures are better predictors of future performance than are their more sensitive counterparts, but the process is still imprecise. Anyone who tells you that you can expect to see a particular level of performance is lying or does not know what he is talking about. If he is trying to sell you something, I strongly suspect the former.

Chapter 13 covers some of the methods you can use to make your trading more robust—that is, less likely to suffer from wild swings in performance.

thirteen

BULLETPROOF SYSTEMS

*Trading is not a sprint; it's boxing. The market will beat you up,
screw with your head, and do anything it can to defeat you.
But when the bell sounds at the end of the twelfth round,
you must be standing in the ring in order to win.*

N ew traders who build trading systems are looking for a single supercharged trading system that demonstrates the best possible results in historical testing. They believe a system that shows superior performance via historical data will indicate similar performance in future trading. They look at tests showing a system (call it Omega) that has a 10 percent better CAGR% and a 0.2 better MAR than another system (call it Alpha) and conclude that they would be foolish to trade with Alpha when Omega seems so much better.

Later, with more experience, one realizes that there is no such thing as a perfect system. The Omega system might perform better in certain types of market conditions, and because of the prevalence of the most favorable conditions in the past the Omega system might have outperformed the Alpha system significantly in testing. Unfortunately, there is no guarantee that those conditions will occur with the same frequency in the future as they did in the past. In other words, the distribution of the types of markets may be different in the future from what it was in the past. So if the performance differences that were shown in testing between Omega and Alpha are a result of the particular distribution of types of markets, those differences could disappear if the distribution is different in the future.

Consider this example. Suppose Omega works much better than Alpha when markets are trending and quiet but Alpha works better when markets are trending and volatile. Now suppose that in the 20-year test that was done there were 13 years in which the trends that occurred were predominantly quiet and 7 years in which the trends were mostly volatile. If the same distribution occurs in the future, Omega will have better performance.

But what if 5 of the 7 years of volatile trends occurred during the last 10 years of testing? What if there were changes in market behavior as a result of trader effects that would result in trends being more volatile in the future? This might indicate that the Alpha system would be more likely to have better performance in the future since it performs better when there are volatile trends. Conversely, what if the market seemed to indicate a likely cyclical shift from quiet to volatile markets and back again? Would this not make it more likely that the Omega system would perform better in the future as the markets shifted back to more quiet trends from the period of recent volatile trends?

The Unknowable Future

In many cases, the reality is that we simply do not have enough information to make these sorts of decisions with any certainty. The reason for this is that we do not have enough data. Consider the sequence QQQVVQ. If this sequence represents the periods of quiet versus volatile markets, can one determine with any reliability the relative probability of future markets being volatile or quiet? If you were paying attention in earlier chapters, you'd realize that a sample size of six is not enough to draw any certain conclusions. Even if we have a larger sequence such as VQQVQVVQQQQVVQ, it may appear that there is a cycle, but there is not enough data for us to make that assessment with any reliability.

In these cases, it is best to come to terms with the fact that we do not have enough data and therefore do not know what the future will bring; therefore, we cannot predict the relative performance of systems in the future accurately except in very broad terms. A mature understanding of this reality is critical to building a robust trading program. As is the case with many aspects of trading, seeing the truth is a crucial first step. Once you see it, you can make decisions that reflect that truth and adjust your actions accordingly.

Robust Trading

Robust trading is about building a trading program that will perform well no matter what the future brings. It is founded on accepting the reality that no one can know the future and that there is a very large margin of error inherent in any testing based on historical data.

Ironically, you will find that your trading performance becomes more predictable, once you build a trading program that takes into account the unknowable nature of the future, The reason for this seeming paradox is simple: If your trading program is built on the premise that the future is unknowable, you are assured that the future will bring conditions that your trading program anticipated, something you did not predict. In contrast, a trading program built on the assumption of a particular set of market characteristics — almost any assumption at all, in fact — will suffer if the conditions on which the program is based are not present.

So how do you build a trading program that is not dependent on particular market conditions? There are two major attributes in any robust trading program: *diversity* and *simplicity*. Nature provides the best example of how these factors increase robustness. A strong analogy can be made between the survival ability of an ecosystem and individual species within that system and the robustness of a trading program.

Diversity

At the level of the ecosystem, nature does not rely on one or two species to perform a task. It does not have only one type of predator, only one food source, only one herbivore, or only one scavenger to clean up the remains of the dead. Diversity is important because it insulates the ecosystem from the effects of radical change in the population of one of the species.

Simplicity

Complex ecosystems are more resilient, and complex species seem to have significant advantages over simpler ones when the environment is stable. However, during times of change, complex species are more likely to die off. At those times, the hardiest species are those which are very simple, such as viruses and bacteria. Simple organisms are hardier because they are less dependent on their specific surroundings. That simplicity is significantly beneficial when the ecosystem is subjected to major change such as that which might occur if a large meteor struck the earth or a large volcano eruption caused a major drop in temperatures. When the climate changes, dependency on the previous climate is a significant *dis*advantage.

Robust Organisms

There are some species that are complex but still are robust, or able to survive in varying conditions. Those species generally developed in climates or conditions where they were subjected to constant change and therefore developed an ability to survive during those changes. Those robust species serve as a model that can be used to develop systems that are robust.

Now that we have considered the two building blocks of robustness in nature—diversity and simplicity—let's examine ways to add them to a trading program. Simplicity can be added by minimizing the rules that create dependencies on specific market conditions. Diversity can be added by trading as many markets as possible that do not correlate with one another. It also can be added by trading many different types of systems at the same time so that no matter what market conditions the future brings, there will be some systems in your portfolio that are performing well.

Robust Systems

The primary ways to make systems more robust is to have rules that allow those systems to adapt to different market conditions and to keep the systems simple and less susceptible to changes in the market.

You can build systems that are more robust by making them adapt to market conditions as those conditions change. This approach is analogous to those complex organisms in nature that are able to survive in varying conditions because of their superior adaptability. A human being is one example. People are able to survive in the deserts of the Sahara and the ice of the Arctic because they have the brain power that allows them to adapt to those very different environments.

Any system will perform better under certain market conditions. Trend-following systems do better when markets are trending and quiet; countertrend systems do better when markets are stable and volatile. A portfolio filter is a rule that can make a system more robust because it can filter out markets when a particular market is not in a state that is favorable for a particular system. The Donchian Trend system, for example, has a portfolio filter. It does not allow trades when the market is breaking out against the trend, as this occurs only when the market is not in a favorable state. A breakout in the direction of the trend occurs more often in trending markets. The addition of this filter makes the system more robust.

In a similar manner, simple rules make systems more robust because those rules work in a greater variety of circumstances. Complex systems generally are complex because they have been designed to take advantage of some conditions or market behavior that was noticed during system development. The more those rules are added, the more the system becomes tied to a more specific set of market conditions and behaviors. This makes it likelier that the future will produce markets that don't have those particular behaviors or in which the rules no longer work as well.

Simple rules that are built on more durable concepts will hold up in actual trading better than will complex rules that are tailored to more specific market behavior. Keep your systems simple and you will find that they hold up better over time.

Market Diversification

One of the most effective ways to improve the robustness of your overall trading is to include a diverse range of markets. If you trade more markets, you increase the chance that you will encounter conditions favorable to your trading system in at least one of those markets. In the case of trend-following systems, if you trade more markets, you boost the odds that for any particular period there will be a trend in one of those markets.

This means that you want to have a portfolio that includes as many markets as possible. The markets should present new opportunities, and so they should not be highly correlated to other markets. For example, there are several short-term U.S. interest-rate products that move almost in lockstep. Adding more than one of these products to your portfolio will not add diversity.

If you are trading systems that do not require close monitoring, you should consider trading foreign markets. Those markets can add a lot of diversification and help make your trading more robust and consistent. Any of the systems shown here that buy on the open based on closing price data will be relatively easy to trade on markets around the world because the time-zone differences are less important if you have to worry about only market closes and opens.

Deciding Which Markets to Trade

At this time, the most popular platform for testing systems, TradeStation, has the extreme limitation of being unable to test more than one market at a time. One side effect of this is that many traders think in terms of markets, not portfolios. This has led to the erroneous belief that some markets should not be included in a trend-following portfolio because those markets are not profitable or because they underperform compared with others.

There are two problems with this perspective. First, trends may happen only every several years in some markets, and so short tests of 5 or 10 years will not show the market's full potential. Second, the benefit of diversification for a market may outweigh any negative profitability.

Consider the cocoa market example from Chapter 4. Recall how that market had a long string of losing trades before there was a good trend. This is very common. Here's an example from my Turtle days that is particularly noteworthy. In the early part of 1985 Rich told us we no longer could trade coffee. I think he felt that there was not enough volume for us to trade it and we had been consistently losing money with it. That decision caused us to lose out on what would have been our single biggest trade (see Figure 13-1).

Since I did not take that trade, I can't tell you exactly what I would have made from memory, and so I performed a test using the data from the March 1986 coffee contract. At the time of entry, the value for N was 1.29 cents. This meant that I would have been trading a unit size of 103 contracts since I traded a $5 million account for all of 1985. Because we traded four units at a time, I would have been long 412 contracts of coffee for that trade. The profit would have been approximately $34,000 per contract. The aggregate profit for the trade would have been 412 times $34,000, or approximately $14 million, representing a 280 percent return on

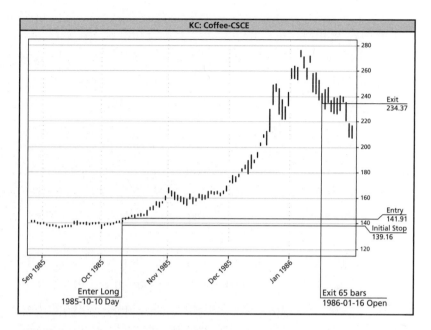

Figure 13-1 The Coffee Trade We Missed

the $5 million account for a single trade. No other trade from the Turtle era came close to being as big as this trade that we missed.

Does this mean that one should trade all markets? Are there no good reasons to exclude particular markets from trading? The primary reason for not trading a particular market is liquidity. Markets that do not have active trading and sufficient volume can be much harder to trade. The more successful you become, the more this becomes a limiting factor. It was the reason Rich kept us out of the coffee trade. When you combined our trading sizes with Rich's, we were trading thousands of contracts in coffee when we entered and exited. That was certainly at the edge of viable volume limits. Therefore, Rich's decision was a very rational one, though one I wished he had not made before the coffee trade discussed above materialized.

You may be thinking that you can trade an illiquid market if you have a small account size. This may be true depending on the type of system you are using, but it may be wrong. The problem with illiquid markets is not that you cannot get in and out most of the time. The problem is that in certain circumstances you can have many orders and no traders to take the other side. Illiquid markets mean few buyers and sellers. So your single contract buy order may be sitting in a pack of 200 to 500 contracts to buy when there are no sellers at all. This does not happen as often in more liquid markets.

Illiquid markets are also more susceptible to price shocks. Take at look at the charts for rough rice, lumber, propane, and any market that trades less than a few thousand shares a day and compare the number of large one-day moves with that in more liquid markets. You will find that there are many more days with large unexpected price moves in the illiquid markets.

Different Types of Markets

There is another reason you might choose to exclude certain markets from your trading. Although I don't believe that one should exclude certain markets because they have not been as profitable as others when tested in a simulation, I do believe that there are some fundamental differences between certain classes of markets that warrant the exclusion of an entire class from trading with a particular class of systems.

Some traders believe that various individual markets are different and should be treated as such. I think the reality is more complicated. I believe that there are actually three classes of markets that behave distinctly differently but that within those classes the differences between markets are attributable largely to random events. The major classes of markets are as follows:

1. **Fundamentals-driven markets.** These are markets such as currencies and interest rates in which the trading is not the primary force behind the movement; larger macroeconomic events and forces drive the price. As time goes on this seems to be less and less true, but I would argue that the Federal Reserve or a country-specific equivalent and a country's monetary policy still influence prices more than do speculators in the currency and interest rate markets. These markets have the greatest liquidity with the cleanest trends and are the easiest for trend followers to trade.

2. **Speculator-driven markets.** These are markets such as stocks and futures such as coffee, gold, silver, and crude oil in which speculators influence the markets more than governments or large hedgers do. The prices are perception-driven. These markets are harder for trend followers to trade.

3. **Aggregated derivative markets.** These are markets in which the driving force is speculation, but that speculation is diluted because the traded instruments are derivative of other markets that are themselves aggregations of individual component stocks. A good example is the e-mini S&P futures contract. It moves up and down, but its range is constrained by the underlying S&P 500 index. The S&P index in turn moves only indirectly because of speculators. Since an index aggregates the purely speculative moves of many stocks, there is an averaging out and a dilution of

momentum. These markets are the hardest ones for trend followers to trade.

My proposition is this: Markets in any of these classes trade the same way. You should trade them or not according to liquidity and class only. As a Turtle I decided not to trade class 3 at all, whereas many of the Turtles chose to trade that class of markets. I felt our systems were not good for derivative aggregated markets. It is not that you can't trade them, just that they just cannot be traded as well with a medium-term breakout trend-following system like the one we traded; so, I never traded the S&P as a Turtle.

Markets in each of the classes behave similarly. Although you certainly will see periods, perhaps years or decades, of differences, you will find that over the long run this is simply the reflection of trader memory and the relative rarity and random nature of underlying fundamental causes for large trends.

Trader Memory

A good example of trader memory is gold and silver. When I first started trading, it was impossible to make any money in gold because the memory of the enormous 1978 trend (when gold went to $900 an ounce and silver went to over $50 an ounce) was still too fresh in people's minds. Every time the price even started to look like a potential up trend, everyone and his brother would start buying gold. That made the price movements very choppy. The price would run up and run down and then run up and run down again. In short, it was very hard to trade as a trend follower. Now, 20 years later, most people do not remember the 1978 trend anymore, and so the move in the spring of 2006 was much easier to trade than it had been earlier; if you looked at the charts, you would say that gold had changed its character.

I do not think one can tell when the next market such as gold is going to change or when the next market such as cocoa is going to trend again. The fact that a market has not had a large trend in the last 20 years does not make it a bad market to trade. For me, if a market has enough volume to trade and is different from the other markets in your portfolio, you should trade that market.

The constraint to market diversification is often the amount of capital required to trade many markets within acceptable risk limits. This is one of the reasons successful hedge fund operators have an easier time than do individual traders and why large traders have more consistent performance than do smaller traders. If you can afford to trade only 10 markets, you can expect more erratic performance than will be the case if you can afford to trade 50 or 60 markets simultaneously. It takes at least $100,000 to trade a long-term trend-following system using futures contracts with reasonable diversification. Even at that level the risk required would be too high for most traders.

System Diversification

In addition to diversifying across markets, you can increase the robustness of your trading program by diversifying your systems. Using more than one system at a time can make a trading program significantly more robust, especially if the systems are significantly different.

Consider two systems. The better one has an RAR% of 38.2 percent with an R-cubed of 1.19, and the worse one has an RAR% of

14.5 percent and an R-cubed of 0.41. If you tested both systems, which one would you trade? Would you trade only the better one? That seems the logical choice.

However, that choice ignores the benefits of diversification when the systems are not correlated. Those benefits are even greater when the systems are negatively correlated (i.e., one tends to make money when the other one is losing money). That is the case with particular systems that provide very significant benefits when they are combined, as you will see below.

Trading both systems at the same time has an RAR% of 61.2 percent and an R-cubed of 5.20. Needless to say, that is a significant improvement over the performance of either system alone.

The systems mentioned above are actually the two parts of the Bollinger Breakout system. The better system trades only long volatility channel breakouts, and the worse system trades only short volatility channel breakouts. It is fairly easy to understand why these systems work well when combined, but the improvement in performance is quite dramatic.

One can get the same benefits by combining systems that work well in different market conditions, such as one that performs well in trending markets and another that works well in markets when there are no trends. When one is suffering a drawdown, the other one may be profitable, and vice versa. This does not always work out as smoothly as one might hope, but you can improve the robustness of your trading program greatly with approaches like this.

As with market diversification, the limit to system diversification is that it often requires significant capital or management effort to trade many systems at the same time. This is one of the reasons successful hedge fund operators have an easier time than do individual traders. It may require $200,000 to diversify a long-term trend-following system adequately. Trading four or five different systems may require as much as $1 million or more. This factor alone may cause many people to decide to place their money with a good professional trader who runs a commodity pool or hedge fund rather than trade for their own accounts privately.

Facing Reality

A robust trading program is built on the premise that you cannot predict the specific market conditions you will encounter in your actual trading. Robust trading accounts for this by building systems that are robust because they are adaptable or simple and are not specifically dependent on market conditions. A mature robust trading program trades many different systems in many different markets and is much more likely to perform consistently in the future than is a program that trades a small number of systems that have been highly tailored to a small number of markets.

MASTERING YOUR DEMONS

The market does not care how you feel. It will not prop up your ego or console you when you are down. Therefore, trading is not for everyone. If you are unwilling to face the truth about the markets and the truth about your own limitations, fears, and failures, you will not succeed.

I hope that some of you may be as inspired by the Turtle story as I was when I first read about the great speculator Jesse Livermore in Edwin Lefèvre's *Reminiscences of a Stock Operator* in 1982. The fact that Richard Dennis was able to teach a group of traders in two weeks and then have them go on to earn more than $100 million for him over the next four years has become one of trading's most compelling stories. The success of the Turtle experiment has proven that Richard had a set of teachable principles that if followed consistently would result in profitable trading.

The funny thing is that most of the principles that Richard Dennis taught us were not new. Some were basic principles that had been espoused by other famous traders since before Richard was born. Yet the very simplicity of the principles we were taught in some respects was a hindrance for those of us who tried to follow them in those initial months.

People have a tendency to believe that complicated ideas are better than simple ones. Many find it hard to comprehend that Richard Dennis could have made several hundred million dollars by using a handful of simple rules. It is natural to think that he must have had some secret. Many of the Turtles fought that demon during our first few months of trading. Some of us thought that trading successfully couldn't possibly be that simple; that there must be something else to it. This type of thinking obstructed some of the Turtles' trading so much that they never were able to follow the straightforward rules Richard had outlined.

My theory is that this belief and the need for complication come from insecurity and the resulting need to find some reason to feel special in some way. Having secret knowledge makes us feel special; possessing simple truths does not. Therefore, our egos drive us to believe that we possess some kind of special knowledge to prove to ourselves that we are somehow superior to others. Our egos don't want us to limit ourselves to commonly known truths. The ego wants secrets.

Live By the Ego, Die By the Ego

This is the major reason why beginning traders are drawn to discretionary trading. Discretionary trading feeds the ego; it is trading that relies on one's judgment, in contrast with systematic trading, where trading decisions are made by using rules that specify *exactly when and how much to buy and sell*. So when you use your judgment to trade and you win, the ego wins. You can then brag to your friends how you are the master of the markets.

I see this particular behavior constantly on online trading forums—especially the broad-based ones that attract new traders. You regularly see posts from individuals bragging about how they bought just before a run-up, or they have found the Holy Grail and have a 90 percent accurate system, or they have been trading for three months and have made 200 percent. They invariably have done this by trading with too much leverage, so they might have turned $5,000 into $15,000; however, they run a very high risk of losing that $15,000 because they are trading too aggressively. A few months later, you may see the same traders post that they have blown up their account and lost everything. These individuals were trading to feed their egos, and as the saying goes, live by the ego, die by the ego.

There are many successful discretionary traders, but there are far more unsuccessful ones. The biggest reason for this is that the ego is not your friend as a trader. The ego wants to be right, it wants to predict, and it wants to know secrets. The ego makes it much more difficult to trade well by avoiding the cognitive biases that hinder profits.

An example from the Turtle days will bring this point home.

The Great Ping-Pong Battle

Some people may find this hard to believe since trading seems like a very exciting job to outsiders, but most of the time when we were trading we did absolutely nothing. We were bored. The markets were quiet most of the time. In short, the Turtles had a lot of free time on their hands.

Fortunately, we had a Ping-Pong table, and so Ping-Pong was our game. Almost all of us played it at least once a day. We played so much that one day we had a note posted to our door from someone in the large insurance office adjacent to ours threatening our deaths because they did not like the fact that we got to play games all day while they had to do work (presumably they did **not** like their work).

I had never played the game seriously before, but I soon developed reasonable skills and started beating some of the better players after a few months. I adopted the Chinese-style pen hold grip, which allowed me to switch between forehand and backhand more easily—that was better for my aggressive spin-filled style.

But there was one Turtle who was much better than any of the rest of us, one we all knew we could not beat. He had been playing for a long time, and we all watched in awe when he played. He generally had no problems beating us 21 to 10 or by an even larger margin, and we knew he was just toying with us. He beat us without breaking a sweat.

After a few months of play, one of the Turtles suggested that we have a tournament. In a group full of competitive traders, this was serious stuff. We all felt that the tournament probably would really be about who was second best since there was no doubt who was the best player; however, we wanted to see who would be champ. When the tournament began, the weaker players were weeded out one by one until we were down to the strongest eight players. With the exception of the best player, we were all pretty close in skills.

I decided to change my style for the tournament. Instead of going for kill shots whenever I had a chance the way I normally did,

I played conservatively. I even changed my grip from the pen hold to the more accurate traditional style (the way one holds a tennis racket) and my paddle from the spongy ones that give lots of spins to the sandpaper ones that are better for defense since they are less responsive to the spin of the opponent. I knew that the best player had superior spin technique and would not have any problem handling my comparatively feeble spins so if I were to do well against him I was better off with a paddle that weakened his advantage of superior spin technique.

My strategy paid off as I slowly beat my next two opponents in close and exciting matches. That meant that we were now down to two players and I would be playing in the championship round against a much superior player, the one we all expected to win the tournament. I would have to play my best game and he would have to break for me to win, and we all knew it. All the Turtles were present for this final match, which pitted youth and energy against experience and skill.

As we started to play, I noticed something: My opponent really wanted to win the match; he was taking it very seriously. It was obvious that it was very important for him to win. He had much to lose since he was already considered the superior player, already counted as the best. In contrast, I had nothing to lose. I already had won the tournament as the rest of us saw it. No one expected me to win or even thought that I could win.

He won the first few points pretty easily, in fact, so easily that I began to worry that I might get shut out, skunked. But as I adapted to his superior speed and shot placement and played extremely defensively, I started to wear him out. He was playing more aggressively than he normally would have because he wanted to finish me off quickly. I was playing more conservatively because I knew it was my only chance. I started to get longer volleys before he won the point, and then I finally started to win points—not many at first but just enough to keep me in the game. As I began to win more and more points, my opponent's play suffered. He started to become angry with himself for letting an inferior player gain any sort of advantage.

Slowly the advantage tipped in my favor, and I started coming back in the second game of the match. I clawed my way back to even and then went on to win that game. So at the end of the first two games we were tied one to one, but the momentum was in my favor with one game to play.

The final game was a battle. We fought back and forth with the game tied and with each of us being one point from victory on several occasions. Finally, I hit the last shot and he missed. In the end, the pressure of the tournament, of proving that he was the better player, got to him and he cracked. He was assuredly the best player. I knew it and he knew it, but in the end that didn't matter, and he lost because he couldn't handle the pressure. The win meant too much to him, and that affected his play.

My superior opponent was also not successful in the Turtle program. I believe this was the case for the same reason that he lost the Ping-Pong tournament. His ego was too tied up in his own trading for him to be able to see that the reasons for his poor performance were inside him. Not coincidentally, the Ping-Pong expert was the same Turtle who believed that Rich had given me secrets that he had not been given. It was too hard for him to see that the reason I was making money when he was losing was that I was trading better than he was because I was focusing on the rules and blotting out any ego issues. He blamed it on not having been given the secrets. He did not want to face the truth.

Humble Pie, The Best Food for Traders

If you want to be a great trader, you must conquer your ego and develop humility. Humility allows you to accept the future as something that is unknowable. Humility will keep you from trying to make predictions. Humility will keep you from taking it personally when a trade goes against you and you exit with a loss. Humility will let you embrace trading that is based on simple concepts because you won't have a need to know secrets so that you can feel special.

Don't Be an Ass

Although I had an easier time than most, perhaps all, of the Turtles, I don't want to give the impression that I am some sort of egoless automaton who was immune to the cognitive biases and a master of my own psychology. I was not. Here's a case in point.

Sometime during our second year we were in a big move, and I once again was loaded with the maximum four units we were allowed as part of the rules. I asked a few of the other Turtles how many units they were in, and several of them did not have the full four-unit position. That meant that they were not making as much money as they should have been. Thus, my asking them about their positions was a bit like rubbing their noses in it.

Later that day, like almost every day, I left to catch a commuter train since I lived in the western suburb of Riverside, Illinois. Several of the other Turtles commuted by train as well, and we all would leave at about the same time. I remember opening the door and entering the hallway to hear one of the guys who had left a bit earlier say to the other something like, "Did you hear him today? What an ass."

The thing is they were right. I had been an ass: the worst kind of ass, the clueless dolt who had been one without realizing it. I had not stopped to consider how my actions were affecting the others. Upon the briefest reflection, it was obvious that I had been cruel to brag about having something that they did not. I am sure that it was all the more bitter to have those careless remarks come from a young punk barely out of high school.

I have thought about that day many times over the last 20-plus years since I overhead that bit of conversation. It was the day that I vowed to try to never be an ass again, to spend a little more time thinking about how what I do and say could affect others before I acted. I also try to be a bit more tolerant of the clueless asses I encounter on occasion, mindful of the fact that I too am one from time to time.

ITS NOT ABOUT ME, ITS ABOUT YOU. A

Finding Consistency

The most important lessons in life are simple yet difficult to execute. In trading, consistency is the key. A systematic trading approach, a thorough understanding of the limitations of that approach, and the tools used to build trading systems can help you be more successful and constant. You must be consistent to trade well. You must be able to execute your plan or the plan has no meaning.

If I had to pick the single X factor most responsible for our success as Turtles, it would be the fact that we were taught by a legendary trader. This knowledge gave us a faith in the methods that Richard taught us, making it much easier for us to follow his rules consistently and persistently. Unless you can find another famous trader to teach you and give you the same confidence, you will have to find that faith on your own. You will have to develop confidence in your methods as well as in your ability to make money over time using those methods.

The best way I know to develop faith in systematic approaches to trading is to explore some systems on your own using trading simulation software. The software will let you look at the past in the same way that actual trading does. You will find the process of researching various trading systems and checking your assumptions against actual market data to be a humbling one. If you start actual trading, you may find it to be much harder than you might have thought. Putting real money on the line is not the same as practicing or paper trading.

If you are considering a career in trading, you must keep one important fact in mind, and that is that I am very unusual. By some freak of biology or upbringing, it was not difficult for me to be consistent in my trading. My psychological makeup made it easy for me to repel cognitive biases. So, although I have seen the effects of psychological breakdown and weakness in traders, I am not the best counselor for anyone who needs help overcoming his particular issues because it is not something that I had to rise above myself.

Another thing to consider is that I am not an expert in trading psychology. For these reasons, although I have been able to observe firsthand the importance of psychological strength, I cannot offer specific advice on how to build it beyond what is contained in this book. Fortunately, there are others who have made a study of such psychology and are able to offer specific advice to those who may have a more difficult time trading than I did. Many have found the writings of Van Tharp, Brett Steenbarger, Ari Kiev, and Mark Douglas helpful in their own efforts to master their trading demons. I encourage you to consider those sources.

Finally, my experience primarily has been as a trend follower. I have explored and traded other styles, including day trading and swing trading, and so I know that the principles outlined in this book apply to those types of trading as well. Do not take my focus on trend following to imply that this is the best way to trade. In fact, trend following is probably *not* for most people. Each style requires a particular psychological makeup that you may or may not possess. Matching your personality with its strengths and weaknesses against a particular trading style is very important, and several of the authors mentioned above can speak more authoritatively on this subject.

Lessons from the Turtles

1. **Trade with an edge:** Find a trading strategy that will produce positive returns over the long run because it has a positive expectation.
2. **Manage risk:** Control risk so that you can continue to trade or you may not be around to see the benefits of a positive expectation system.

3. **Be consistent:** Execute your plan consistently to achieve the positive expectation of your system.
4. **Keep it simple:** Simple systems hold up better over time than do more complex ones.

Remember that a plan means nothing if it is not acted on. If you really want to be a successful trader, commit yourself to the first step. I did, and I've never regretted it.

WHEN ALL IS
SAID AND DONE

Two roads diverged in a wood, and I—
I took the one less traveled by,
And that has made all the difference.
—Robert Frost

I spent a great deal of time over the last few months focusing on the first part of this book because I wanted it be an apt introduction to the epilogue. It was this last chapter that I was most enthusiastic about completing.

Once you have lived the life of a trader—lived as a Turtle—the trader's philosophy permeates the rest of your experience. As you work through and see your way around cognitive biases and make adjustments for them in your thinking as it relates to the markets, you start to do the same thing in other areas of your life. One of the ways in which good traders differ from those who are less successful is that they are not afraid to be different, to do something unlike what everyone else is doing, to take their own path.

Take Your Own Path

I was 19 years old when I decided to become a trader. I was confident of my potential success and told some of my closest friends that I would be a millionaire by age 21. I was not bragging as much as sharing my hope for being successful in trading. It was new to me, and it fascinated me. I made a commitment to trading even though that meant dropping out of college. My father, who did not have a college degree and felt that had held him back in his career, was not pleased. But I have always been an individualist, unafraid to voice my opinions, unafraid to disagree with authority, and so I did not really care what everyone else thought; I knew it was the right decision for me. My independence and outspokenness have gotten me into trouble at times; I'm sure this has worried my mother on numerous occasions, but it has served me well.

It is hard to imagine what life would have been like if I had not decided to drop everything else to become a trader. I certainly would not have responded to Richard Dennis's ad in the paper.

Now I see life as a trader approaches his craft: Nothing ventured, nothing gained. Risk is your friend. Don't be afraid of it. Understand it. Control it. Dance with it. Traders take chances with good expectation but expect to lose regularly. They are not hesitant to act because they're afraid that they might be wrong, a quality that emerges in the kind of life they lead. They follow their own path and don't worry that sometimes they will fail in certain attempts because they know that is part of life; they understand that failure is a necessary prerequisite to success and learning.

I always have enjoyed extreme challenges and attempted to do things that most people consider foolish, impractical, or impossible. I see possibilities where many people see obstacles and am compelled to pursue those opportunities. I have failed in this many times, but I also have succeeded with each experience and learned something new.

If people asked me what my goal was, I would answer: "To make the world a better place, of course." I think the power lies in all of us to make the world better in some concrete way, however small. That is a worthy objective. I would be far richer and more "successful" if I had stuck to trading and never ventured into anything new. Some of the other Turtles did that and have been wildly successful running hedge funds with hundreds of millions or even billions of dollars under management. Similarly, if I had stuck with a particular niche in the software industry, I might be more successful, at least as others measure success.

True to my nature, I don't care about others' opinions of my success. They are not going to be the ones at my deathbed wondering whether I made a difference, whether I lived well and fully. I am.

The Track to Nowhere

Most of my oldest friends think I am going through some sort of prolonged midlife crisis. I probably seem irresponsible and unconventional to them. If having a midlife crisis means examining your life and deciding that you don't want to live by a set of success criteria created by society and the media, I am guilty as charged. I highly recommend having one if you haven't done so already. The alternative is much less interesting.

I constantly meet people who have lost themselves in an empty pursuit of what they ought to do. In an effort to please their parents and teachers, to get a *good* job, to make a *lot* of money, and so on, they followed a path set out by others rather than one they chose for themselves. For some, this started in grammar school; for others, it happened as late as college or perhaps shortly after they started their first real jobs and began to take on responsibilities. Invariably, the path took them far from their dreams and what they had hoped they would become. They lost sight of the fact that they had a choice: They could decide at any time to do something else—decide perhaps to step off the path and explore the world and themselves a bit.

In many companies there is a word for this path. It is called a *career track*, or *track* for short. That is a good analogy because a train engineer cannot decide what route to take; those decisions are made by the people who set out the track and those who control the switches along the way. I have been thinking about this phenomenon quite a bit lately, and it occurs to me that the reason most people don't follow their dreams is that they are afraid of failing in their endeavors. They believe it is better to follow a predetermined path that they know they can achieve rather than one of their own making where they will be tested.

I don't believe that anyone consciously makes this decision; it happens by default or through lack of action. People do not say to themselves: "I'd really like a boring job working for a company I hate." It just happens.

They step onto the track without realizing it. Then, once they are on it, it takes a conscious effort to leave it. Otherwise they will end up wherever it leads, which is probably not where they wanted to go. Since they did not step consciously onto the track, they may not even realize where they are until they find themselves very far away from their dreams.

Our individual accomplishments are limited far more by the bounds of what we consider to be impossible than by objective reality. If we don't take a certain step because we don't believe we will succeed, we have placed a barrier in front of that success that is far stronger than reality. If we try, we may fail—but we may succeed. If we never try at all, we make it impossible to succeed.

Learning Requires Failure

Besides, failure is not so bad. The Dalai Lama has said that you should thank your enemies because they teach you more than your friends and family do. Failure is one such enemy, and a very powerful one at that. I know because I have failed more often and in a greater variety of attempts than anyone I know. I also have had some spectacular successes that I would not have experienced if I had not been willing to risk failing. I'll take that a step further and admit that I've learned far more from my mistakes and failures than from any of my accomplishments. You cannot learn without risking failure. That's part of the reason I've experienced my share of failure: I like to learn new things. Learning requires failure; you won't learn if you are not willing to make mistakes and fail.

Most people believe that as we get older it gets harder to learn, that our brains change somehow. They point to children and how quickly they learn to speak a new language and contrast that with how hard it is for adults to learn a new language, crediting youth as the X factor. I believe the big difference in the ability for children to learn a new language as opposed to adults is that kids are not afraid of sounding foolish or of making mistakes in grammar and pronunciation while adults are terrified of this.

I recently moved to Buenos Aires, Argentina and have become friendly with a number of students of all ages and nationalities who are here to study Spanish. One of the most interesting things I have noticed is that some who have been in the country for only a few months or weeks are able to converse at a basic level even though they did not have any background in the language before their arrival. Others may have studied Spanish for years in school but cannot speak conversationally even after several weeks of intensive classes and residence in Buenos Aires.

This difference in learning is due almost entirely to the degree of fear they feel about making mistakes or sounding foolish. Some do not care how they sound; they just start conversing. They realize that everyone who learns a language errs at times and that this is part of the process. They let themselves fail and improve with the experience. Each time someone looks at them with a blank stare in response to what was said, they learn. They learn each time they order a meal and do not get what they thought they had requested. These students do so well at failing *and learning* that they now can converse fluently in Spanish, and they will continue to improve their speaking skills with daily practice.

Changing Paths

If you find yourself on the wrong path—a track leading you somewhere you don't want to go—keep in mind our discussion of the sunk cost effect. Do not worry about how much time you've spent on a career you don't like or how much you have invested in a relationship that you know will not work. A trader knows not to hide from reality. She knows that when the market indicates that a trade is not working, that is not the time to *hope* for a change, wish that things were different, or pretend that reality is different; it is the time to exit the trade.

Reality has a way of persisting despite our best attempts to wish it away. Turtles embrace reality rather than trying to avoid it. This makes it easier to change directions when we find that things are not as we hoped or expected. We don't complain, we don't worry, we don't hope; we do something concrete to adjust to our new perception of reality.

On Money

I think it is easier to make a lot of money if you don't really want it badly. This is especially true for traders. I remember that one of the Turtles was strongly affected by the large fluctuations in equity that would come from market moves when we had large positions. Making a lot of money was very important to him. At one point I returned from vacation and found out that he had destroyed his telephone because he was so angry that the market had moved against us.

I don't think it was a coincidence that he had trouble following the system. I think that his desire to make a lot of money made it harder for him to execute the systems we were trading consistently. I was successful at least partly because I did not care about the money. I cared about trading well. I cared what Rich thought of my trading, but I didn't care about the money that was flowing in and out of my account each day.

Money is a tool; it is necessary for certain things. It is very useful, but it is a very poor objective in and of itself. Being wealthy does not make you happy. I know. I have tried it several times.

I have also tried the opposite. At one point, when I was 33, the stock in a company I founded and took public but no longer worked at dropped suddenly. That meant that my liquid assets dried up almost overnight. I had divorced recently and did not have many other assets besides stock in that company; I had given my house to my wife in the divorce.

I was no longer part of the company I had founded and did not have any faith in the management. Therefore, I no longer viewed myself as an investor but instead as a trader. In my role as a trader, the price had been going down, and so I had been selling. Unfortunately, the market was very thin and the market makers were not the best. Further, I had sufficient shares to drive the price down to close to zero on just my own selling if I was not careful. Therefore, I had been selling 10,000 to 20,000 shares every few weeks for several months before the rapid decline in price.

I was working on a start-up airline at the time and had been using the money from the sales of the stock for costs associated with the start-up and my living expenses. That was no longer an option. I went from having several years' expenses covered to less than two months almost overnight, meaning that I needed to find a way to make money; I needed to get a job. I had not worked for anyone else since the Turtle days. In fact, with the exception of Richard Dennis and my first programming job in high school and college, I never had worked for someone else. I spent several months looking for a job that was interesting and landed a consulting job working on a marketing project for a small Internet start-up. I was literally out of cash at that point and barely managed to find enough money to pay for the hotel I stayed in until I cashed my first paycheck.

Some might have considered this a terrible experience, but I didn't. The things I really enjoyed in life were not affected much by my change in condition. I liked to go out with friends to lunch and dinner, have discussions with interesting people, talk about doing something challenging with a group of people, and the like. None of those activities required much money, and I was more able to do them in my new job in Silicon Valley than I had been able to do in Lake Tahoe or Reno, where I had lived previously. I was actually having more fun and enjoying my life as much as or more than I had when I had had millions because I was able to do something that I really loved.

That experience also gave me greater empathy for those who do not have money or are in poor circumstances. I now know what it is like not to be able to eat when hungry and to live from paycheck to paycheck.

I also learned a tremendous amount about start-ups and entrepreneurial management during that period. I had not realized it, but not having worked for anyone else had been a significant disadvantage. It is certainly more difficult to manage people well when you don't know what it is like to be managed yourself. As a consultant, I was at the bottom of the organization chart. I had no direct reports or even the silly little perks that employees get, which somehow seemed important since they were not available to me. I also had no real power. I could effect change only through influence. That was a disadvantage, but it forced me to hone my skills of persuasion, and I was able to effect some changes when people believed in my perspective. Since it was a bigger challenge to effect change with no real power, I enjoyed it immensely.

I believe that the lessons and skills I learned in that period have been invaluable and will continue to help me in my future efforts. I have experienced things that many people fear; I feared those things myself. In every case the reality of what I feared was never as bad as the fear itself.

I say this to encourage you to chase your dreams, even those you may have given up on. If you fail in the attempt, learn from that failure and try again. If you persist, you will move closer and closer to your goal, or you may find that another goal becomes even more important.

Go ahead and take that trade. It may not turn out the way you expected or hoped, but then again, it may turn out even better. You will never know if you don't try.

ORIGINAL TURTLE
TRADING RULES

I always say that you could publish my trading rules in the newspaper and no one would follow them. The key is consistency and discipline. Almost anybody can make up a list of rules that are 80% as good as what we taught our people. What they couldn't do is give them the confidence to stick to those rules even when things are going bad.
—Richard Dennis, quoted in *Market Wizards* by Jack D. Schwager

A Complete Trading System

Most successful traders use a mechanical trading system. This is not a coincidence. A good mechanical trading system automates the entire process of trading. The system provides answers for each of the decisions a trader must make while trading. It makes it easier for a trader to trade consistently because there is a set of rules that specifically define exactly what should be done. The mechanics of trading are not left up to the judgment of the trader.

If you know that your system makes money over the long run, it is easier to take the signals and trade according to the system during periods of losses. If you are relying on your own judgment when you are trading, you may find that you are fearful when you should be bold and courageous when you should be cautious.

If you have a mechanical trading system that works and follow it consistently, your trading will be consistent despite the inner emotional struggles that may result from a long series of losses or a large profit. The confidence, consistency, and discipline afforded by a thoroughly tested mechanical system are the key to many of the most profitable traders' success.

The Turtle Trading System was a *complete* trading system. Its rules covered every aspect of trading and left no decisions to the subjective whims of the trader. It had every component of a complete trading system that covers each of the decisions required for successful trading:

- **Markets:** What to buy or sell
- **Position Sizing:** How much to buy or sell
- **Entries:** When to buy or sell
- **Stops:** When to get out of a losing position
- **Exits:** When to get out of a winning position
- **Tactics:** How to buy or sell

Markets: What to Buy or Sell

The first decision is what to buy and sell or, essentially, what markets to trade. If you trade too few markets, you greatly reduce your chances of getting aboard a trend. At the same time, you do not want to trade markets that have too low a trading volume or that do not trend well.

Position Sizing: How Much to Buy or Sell

The decision about how much to buy or sell is fundamental, yet it often is glossed over or handled improperly by most traders.

How much to buy or sell affects both diversification and money management. Diversification is an attempt to spread risk across many instruments and increase the opportunity for profit by increasing the opportunities for catching successful trades. Proper diversification requires making similar, if not identical, bets on many different instruments. Money management is really about controlling risk by not betting so much that you run out of money before the good trends come.

How much to buy or sell is the single most important aspect of trading. Most beginning traders risk far too much on each trade and greatly increase their chances of going bust even if they have an otherwise valid trading style.

Entries: When to Buy or Sell

The decision about when to buy or sell often is called the entry decision. Automated systems generate entry signals that define the exact price and market conditions that tell you when to enter the market whether by buying or by selling.

Stops: When to Get Out of a Losing Position

Traders who do not cut their losses will not be successful in the long term. The most important thing about cutting your losses is to predefine the point at which you will get out before you enter a position.

Exits: When to Get Out of a Winning Position

Many "trading systems" that are sold as complete systems do not specifically address the exit of winning positions. However, the question of when to get out of a winning position is crucial to the profitability of the system. Any trading system that does not address the exit of winning positions is not a complete system.

Tactics: How to Buy or Sell

Once a signal has been generated, tactical considerations regarding the mechanics of execution become important. This is especially true for larger accounts, where the entry into and exit of positions can result in significant adverse price movement, or market impact.

Using a mechanical system is the best way to make money consistently in trading. If you know that your system makes money over the long run, it is easier to take the signals and follow the system during periods of losses. It is worth repeating that if you rely on your own judgment, during trading you may find that you are fearful when you should be courageous or courageous when you should be fearful.

If you have a profitable mechanical trading system and follow it religiously, your trading will be profitable and the system will help you survive the emotional struggles that inevitably result from a long series of losses or large profits.

The trading system that was used by the Turtles was a complete trading system, and that was a major factor in our success. Our system made it easier to trade consistently and successfully because it did not leave important decisions to the discretion of the trader.

Markets: What the Turtles Traded

The Turtles were futures traders, at the time more popularly called *commodities traders*. We traded futures contracts on the most popular U.S. commodities exchanges. Since we were trading millions of dollars, we could not trade markets that had only a few hundred contracts per day because that would mean that the orders we generated would move the market so much that it would be too difficult to enter and exit positions without taking large losses. The Turtles traded only the most liquid markets. In fact, market liquidity was the primary criterion Richard Dennis used when determining which markets we were to trade.

In general, the Turtles traded all liquid U.S. markets except the grains and the meats. Since Richard Dennis already was trading the full legal position limits for his own account, he could not permit us to trade grains for him without exceeding the exchange's position limits. We did not trade the meats because of a corruption problem with the floor traders in the meat pits. Some years after the Turtles disbanded, the FBI conducted a major sting operation in the Chicago meat pits and indicted many traders for price manipulation and other forms of corruption.

The following is a list of the futures markets traded by the Turtles:

Chicago Board of Trade
- 30-year U.S. Treasury bond
- 10-year U.S. Treasury note

New York Coffee Cocoa and Sugar Exchange
- Coffee

- Cocoa
- Sugar
- Cotton

Chicago Mercantile Exchange

- Swiss franc
- Deutschmark
- British pound
- French franc
- Japanese yen
- Canadian dollar
- S&P 500 stock index
- Eurodollar
- 90-day U.S. Treasury bill

Comex

- Gold
- Silver
- Copper

New York Mercantile Exchange

- Crude oil
- Heating oil
- Unleaded gas

The Turtles were given the discretion of not trading any of the commodities on the list. However, if a trader chose not to trade a particular market, he was not to trade that market at all. We were not supposed to trade markets inconsistently.

Position Sizing

The Turtles used a position sizing algorithm that was very advanced for its day because it normalized the dollar volatility of a position by adjusting the position size on the basis of the dollar volatility of the market. That meant that a specific position would tend to move up or down on a specific day about the same amount in dollar terms (compared with positions in other markets) regardless of the underlying volatility of that particular market.

This was done because positions in markets that moved up and down a large amount per contract would have an offsetting smaller number of contracts than would positions in markets that had lower volatility.

This volatility normalization was very important because it meant that different trades in different markets tended to have the same chance for a particular dollar loss or a particular dollar gain. This increased the effectiveness of the diversification of trading across many markets.

Even if the volatility of a specific market was lower, any significant trend would result in a sizable win because the Turtles would have held more contracts of that lower volatility commodity.

Volatility: The Meaning of *N*

The Turtles used a concept that Richard Dennis and Bill Eckhardt called N to represent the underlying volatility of a particular market. N is simply the 20-day exponential moving average of the true range, which is now more commonly known as the Average True

Range (or ATR). Conceptually, N represents the average range in price movement that a particular market experiences in a single day, accounting for opening gaps. N was measured in the same points as the underlying contract.

To compute the daily true range, one uses the following relationship:

$$\text{True range} = \text{maximum}(H - L, H - PDC, PDC - L)$$

where

H = current high

L = current low

PDC = previous day's close

To compute N, one can use the following formula:

$$N = \frac{(19 \times PDN + TR)}{20}$$

where

PDN = previous day's N

TR = current day's true range

Since this formula requires a previous day's N value, you must start with a 20-day simple average of the true range for the initial calculation.

Dollar Volatility Adjustment

The first step in determining the position size was to determine the dollar volatility represented by the underlying market's price volatility (defined by its N).

This sounds more complicated than it is. It is determined by using the following simple formula:

$$\text{Dollar volatility} = N \times \text{dollars per point}$$

Volatility-Adjusted Position Units

The Turtles built positions in pieces that we called units. Units were sized so that 1N represented 1 percent of the account equity.

Thus, the unit size for a specific market or commodity can be calculated by using the following formula:

$$\text{Unit size} = \frac{1\% \text{ of account}}{\text{market dollar volatility}}$$

or

$$\text{Unit size} = \frac{1\% \text{ of account}}{N \times \text{dollars per point}}$$

Following are some examples.

Heating Oil HO03H

Consider the following prices, true range, and N values for March 2003 heating oil:

Date	High	Low	Close	True Range	N
11/1/2002	0.7220	0.7124	0.7124	0.0096	0.0134
11/4/2002	0.7170	0.7073	0.7073	0.0097	0.0132
11/5/2002	0.7099	0.6923	0.6923	0.0176	0.0134
11/6/2002	0.6930	0.6800	0.6838	0.0130	0.0134
11/7/2002	0.6960	0.6736	0.6736	0.0224	0.0139
11/8/2002	0.6820	0.6706	0.6706	0.0114	0.0137
11/11/2002	0.6820	0.6710	0.6710	0.0114	0.0136

(continued on next page)

Date	High	Low	Close	True Range	N
11/12/2002	0.6795	0.6720	0.6744	0.0085	0.0134
11/13/2002	0.6760	0.6550	0.6616	0.0210	0.0138
11/14/2002	0.6650	0.6585	0.6627	0.0065	0.0134
11/15/2002	0.6701	0.6620	0.6701	0.0081	0.0131
11/18/2002	0.6965	0.6750	0.6965	0.0264	0.0138
11/19/2002	0.7065	0.6944	0.6944	0.0121	0.0137
11/20/2002	0.7115	0.6944	0.7087	0.0171	0.0139
11/21/2002	0.7168	0.7100	0.7124	0.0081	0.0136
11/22/2002	0.7265	0.7120	0.7265	0.0145	0.0136
11/25/2002	0.7265	0.7098	0.7098	0.0167	0.0138
11/26/2002	0.7184	0.7110	0.7184	0.0086	0.0135
11/27/2002	0.7280	0.7200	0.7228	0.0096	0.0133
12/2/2002	0.7375	0.7227	0.7359	0.0148	0.0134
12/3/2002	0.7447	0.7310	0.7389	0.0137	0.0134
12/4/2002	0.7420	0.7140	0.7162	0.0280	0.0141

The unit size for December 6, 2002, using the N value of 0.0141 from December 4, is as follows:

Heating oil:
N = 0.0141
Account size = $1,000,000
Dollars per point = 42,000 (42,000-gallon contracts with price quoted in dollars)

$$\text{Unit size} = \frac{0.01 \times \$1,000,000}{0.0141 \times 42,000} = 16.88$$

Since it is not possible to trade partial contracts, this would be truncated to an even 16 contracts.

You might ask: "How often is it necessary to compute the values for N and the unit size?" The Turtles were provided with a unit size sheet on Monday of each week that listed N and the unit size in contracts for each of the futures that we traded.

The Importance of Position Sizing

Diversification is an attempt to spread risk across many instruments and increase the opportunity for profit by increasing the opportunities to catch successful trades. To diversify properly requires making similar if not identical bets on many different instruments.

The Turtle System used market volatility to measure the risk involved in each market. We then used that risk measurement to build positions in increments that represented a constant amount of risk (or volatility). That enhanced the benefits of diversification and increased the likelihood that winning trades would offset losing trades.

Note that this diversification is much harder to achieve when one is using insufficient trading capital. Consider the above example if a $100,000 account had been used. The unit size would have been a single contract, since 1.688 truncates to 1. For smaller accounts, the granularity of the adjustment is too large, and this greatly reduces the effectiveness of diversification.

Units as a Measure of Risk

Since the Turtles used the unit as the base measure for position size and since those units were adjusted for volatility risk, the unit was a measure of the risk both of a position and of the entire portfolio of positions.

The Turtles were given risk management rules that limited the number of units that we could maintain at any specific time on four different levels. In essence, those rules controlled the total risk that a trader could carry, and those limits minimized losses during prolonged losing periods as well as during extraordinary price movements.

An example of an extraordinary price movement was the day after the October 1987 stock market crash. The U.S. Federal Reserve lowered interest rates by several percentage points overnight to boost the confidence of the stock market and the country. The Turtles were loaded short in interest-rate futures: eurodollars, T-bills, and bonds. The losses the next day were enormous. In most cases, 40 to 60 percent of account equity was lost in a single day. However, those losses would have been correspondingly higher without the maximum position limits.

The limits were as follows:

Level	Type	Maximum Units
1	Single market	4
2	Closely correlated markets	6
3	Loosely correlated markets	10
4	Single direction, long or short	12

Single markets: A maximum of 4 units per market.

Closely correlated markets: For markets that were closely correlated, there could be a maximum of 6 units in one particular direction (i.e., 6 long units or 6 short units). Closely correlated market groups include heating oil and crude oil; gold and silver; the currencies as a group; interest rate futures such as T-bills and eurodollars; and so on.

Loosely correlated markets: For loosely correlated markets, there could be a maximum of 10 units in one particular direction. Loosely correlated markets included gold and copper; silver and copper; and many grain combinations that the Turtles did not trade because of position limits.

Single direction: The maximum number of total units in one direction long or short was 12 units. Thus, one theoretically could have had 12 units long and 12 units short at the same time.

The Turtles used the term *loaded* to represent having the maximum permitted number of units for a particular risk level. Thus, loaded in yen meant having the maximum 4 units of Japanese yen contracts, completely loaded meant having 12 units, and so forth.

Adjusting Trading Size

There are times when the market does not trend for many months. During those times, it is possible to lose a significant percentage of the equity of the account.

After large winning trades close out, one may want to increase the size of the equity used to compute position size.

The Turtles did not trade normal accounts with a running balance based on the initial equity. We were given notional accounts with a starting equity of zero and a specific account size. For example, many Turtles received a notional account size of $1 million when we started trading in February 1983. That account size was adjusted each year at the beginning of the year. It was adjusted up or down depending on the success of the trader as measured subjectively by Rich. The increase or decrease typically represented something close to the addition of the gains or losses that were made in the account during the preceding year.

The Turtles were instructed to decrease the size of the notional account by 20 percent each time we went down 10 percent of the original account. Thus, if a Turtle trading a $1,000,000 account ever was down 10 percent, or $100,000, we would begin trading as if we had an $800,000 account until we reached the yearly starting equity. If we lost another 10 percent (10 percent of $800,000 or $80,000, for a total loss of $180,000), we would reduce the account size by another 20 percent for a notional account size of $640,000.

There are other, perhaps better strategies for reducing or increasing equity as the account goes up or down. These are the rules that the Turtles used.

Entries

The typical trader thinks mostly in terms of the entry signals when she is thinking about a particular trading system. Traders believe that the entry is the most important aspect of any trading system.

They might be surprised to find that the Turtles used a very simple entry system based on the channel breakout systems taught by Richard Donchian.

The Turtles were given rules for two different but related breakout systems we called System 1 and System 2. We were given full discretion to allocate as much of our equity to either system as we wanted. Some of us chose to trade all our equity using System 2, some chose to use a 50 percent System 1 and 50 percent System 2 split, and others chose different mixes. The two systems were as follows:

System 1: a shorter-term system based on a 20-day breakout

System 2: a simpler long-term system based on a 55-day breakout.

Breakouts

A breakout is defined as the price exceeding the high or low of a particular number of days. Thus, a 20-day breakout would be defined as exceeding the high or low of the preceding 20 days.

Turtles always traded at the breakout when it was exceeded during the day and did not wait until the daily close or the open of the following day. In the case of opening gaps, the Turtles would enter positions on the open if a market opened through the price of the breakout.

System 1 Entry

Turtles entered positions when the price exceeded by a single tick the high or low of the preceding 20 days. If the price exceeded the 20-day high, the Turtles would buy 1 unit to initiate a long position in the corresponding commodity. If the price dropped one tick below the low of the last 20 days, the Turtles would sell 1 unit to initiate a short position.

System 1 breakout entry signals would be ignored if the last breakout would have resulted in a winning trade. *Note:* For the purposes of this test, the last breakout was considered the last breakout in the particular commodity regardless of whether that particular breakout was actually taken or was skipped because of this rule. This breakout would be considered a losing breakout if the price subsequent to the date of the breakout moved 2N against the position before a profitable 10-day exit occurred.

The direction of the last breakout was irrelevant to this rule. Thus, a losing long breakout or a losing short breakout would enable the subsequent new breakout to be taken as a valid entry regardless of its direction (long or short).

However, if a System 1 entry breakout was skipped because the previous trade had been a winner, an entry would be made at the 55-day breakout to avoid missing major moves. This 55-day breakout was considered the failsafe breakout point.

At any given point, if a trader was out of the market, there would always be some price that would trigger a short entry and another different and higher price that would trigger a long entry. If the last breakout was a loser, the entry signal would be closer to the current price (i.e., the 20-day breakout) than it would be if it had been a winner, in which case the entry signal probably would be farther away, at the 55 day breakout.

System 2 Entry

We entered when the price exceeded by a single tick the high or low of the preceding 55 days. If the price exceeded the 55-day high, the Turtles would buy 1 unit to initiate a long position in the corresponding commodity. If the price dropped one tick below the low of the last 55 days, the Turtles would sell 1 unit to initiate a short position.

All breakouts for System 2 would be taken whether or not the previous breakout had been a winner.

Adding Units

Turtles entered single-unit long positions at the breakouts and added to those positions at ½N intervals after their initial entry. This

½N interval was based on the actual fill price of the previous order. Thus, if an initial breakout order slipped by ½N, the new order would be 1 full N past the breakout to account for the ½N slippage, plus the normal ½N unit add interval.

This would continue right up to the maximum permitted number of units. If the market moved quickly enough, it was possible to add the maximum 4 units in a single day.

Here is an example.

Gold

$N = 2.50$

55-day breakout $= 310$

First unit added	310.00
Second unit	310.00 + ½ 2.50, or 311.25
Third unit	311.25 + ½ 2.50, or 312.50
Fourth unit	312.50 + ½ 2.50, or 313.75

Crude Oil

$N = 1.20$

55-day breakout $= 28.30$

First unit added	28.30
Second unit	28.30 + ½ 1.20, or 28.90
Third unit	28.90 + ½ 1.20, or 29.50
Fourth unit	29.50 + ½ 1.20, or 30.10

Consistency

The Turtles were told to be very consistent in taking entry signals because most of the profits in a particular year might come from only two or three large winning trades. If a signal was skipped or missed, this could have a great effect on the returns for the year.

The Turtles with the best trading records consistently applied the entry rules. The Turtles with the worst records and all those who were dropped from the program failed to enter positions consistently when the rules indicated.

Stops

There is an expression: "There are old traders and there are bold traders, but there are no old bold traders." Most traders who do not use stops go broke. The Turtles always used stops.

For most people, it is far easier to cling to the hope that a losing trade will turn around than it is to get out of a losing position and admit that the trade did not work out.

Let me make one thing very clear: Getting out of a losing position when the rules of a system dictate doing that is critical. Traders who do not cut their losses will not be successful in the long term. Almost all the examples of trading that got out of control and jeopardized the health of the financial institution, such as Barings and Long-Term Capital Management, involved trades that were allowed to develop into large losses because they were not cut short when they were small losses.

The most important thing about cutting your losses is to have predefined the point where you will get out before you enter a position. If the market moves to your price, you must get out, no exceptions, every single time. Wavering from this method eventually will result in disaster.

Note: The reader may have noticed an inconsistency between my comments here and those in Chapter 10, where I noted that adding stops sometimes harms system performance and is not always necessary. The systems outlined previously which work well without stops do have an implicit stop because as the price moves against the position there will come a point where the moving averages will cross and the losses will be limited. So in a sense, there is a stop, it is just not one that is visible or known to the trader. For most people, however, the psychological comfort of having a price point where they will exit a losing trade is important. This is especially true of beginners. It can be psychologically destabilizing to watch a position go against you without having a clear view of the point where the pain will end.

Turtle Stops

Having stops did not mean that the Turtles always had actual stop orders placed with the broker.

Since the Turtles carried such large positions, we did not want to reveal our positions or our trading strategies by placing stop orders with brokers. Instead, we were encouraged to have a particular price that when hit would cause us to exit our positions by using either limit orders or market orders.

These stops were nonnegotiable exits. If a particular commodity traded at the stop price, the position was exited each time, every time, without fail.

Stop Placement

The Turtles placed their stops on the basis of position risk. No trade could incur more than 2 percent risk.

Since 1N of price movement represented 1 percent of account equity, the maximum stop that would allow 2 percent risk would be 2N of price movement. Turtles' stops were set at 2N below the entry for long positions and 2N above the entry for short positions.

To keep total position risk at a minimum, if additional units were added, the stops for earlier units were raised by ½N. This generally meant that all the stops for the entire position would be placed at 2N from the most recently added unit. However, in cases in which later units were placed at larger spacing because of either fast markets causing skid or opening gaps, there would be differences in the stops.

Here is an example.

Crude Oil
$N = 1.20$
55-day breakout = 28.30

	Entry Price	Stop
First unit	28.30	25.90

	Entry Price	Stop
First unit	28.30	26.50
Second unit	28.90	26.50

	Entry Price	Stop
First unit	28.30	27.10
Second unit	28.90	27.10
Third unit	29.50	27.10

	Entry Price	Stop
First unit	28.30	27.70
Second unit	28.90	27.70

Third unit	29.50	27.70
Fourth unit	30.10	27.70

Here is a case in which a fourth unit was added at a higher price because the market opened gapping up to 30.80:

	Entry Price	Stop
First unit	28.30	27.70
Second unit	28.90	27.70
Third unit	29.50	27.70
Fourth unit	30.80	28.40

Alternative Stop Strategy: The Whipsaw

The Turtles were told about an alternative stop strategy that resulted in better profitability but was harder to execute because it incurred many more losses, which resulted in a lower win/loss ratio. This strategy was called *the Whipsaw*.

Instead of taking a 2 percent risk on each trade, the stops were placed at ½N for ½ percent account risk. If a particular unit was stopped out, the unit would be reentered if the market reached the original entry price. A few Turtles used this method with good success.

The Whipsaw also had the added benefit of not requiring the movement of stops for earlier units as new units were added, since the total risk would never exceed 2 percent at the maximum 4 units.

For example, using Whipsaw stops, the crude oil entry stops would be as follows:

Crude Oil

$N = 1.20$

55-day breakout $= 28.30$

	Entry Price	Stop
First unit	28.30	27.70

	Entry Price	Stop
First unit	28.30	27.70
Second unit	28.90	28.30

	Entry Price	Stop
First unit	28.30	27.70
Second unit	28.90	28.30
Third unit	29.50	28.90

	Entry Price	Stop
First unit	28.30	27.70
Second unit	28.90	28.30
Third unit	29.50	28.90
Fourth unit	30.10	29.50

Benefits of the Turtle System Stops

Since the Turtles' stops were based on N, they adjusted for the volatility of the markets. More volatile markets would have wider stops, but they also would have fewer contracts per unit. This equalized the risk across all entries and resulted in better diversification and more robust risk management.

Exits

There is another old saying: "You can never go broke taking a profit." The Turtles would not agree with this statement. Getting out of winning positions too early, that is, "taking a profit" too early, is one of the most common mistakes in trading with trend-following systems.

Prices never go straight up; therefore, it is necessary to let the prices go against you if you are going to ride a trend. Early in a trend, this often can mean watching decent profits of 10 to 30 percent fade to a small loss. In the middle of a trend, it may mean watching a profit of 80 to 100 percent drop by 30 to 40 percent. The temptation to lighten the position to "lock in profits" can be very great.

The Turtles knew that where you took a profit could make the difference between winning and losing.

The Turtle System enters on breakouts. Most breakouts do not result in trends. This means that most of the trades that the Turtles made resulted in losses. If the winning trades did not earn enough on average to offset those losses, the Turtles would have lost money. Every profitable trading system has a different optimal exit point.

Consider the Turtle System: If you exit winning positions at a 1N profit and exit losing positions at a 2N loss, you will need twice as many winners to offset the losses from the losing trades.

There is a complex relationship among the components of a trading system. This means that you cannot consider the proper exit for a profitable position without considering the entry, money management, and other factors.

The proper exit for winning positions is one of the most important aspects of trading and the least appreciated. However, it can make the difference between winning and losing.

Turtle Exits

The System 1 exit was a 10-day low for long positions and a 10-day high for short positions. All the units in the position would be exited if the price went against the position for a 10-day breakout.

The System 2 exit was a 20-day low for long positions and a 20-day high for short positions. All the units in the position would be exited if the price went against the position for a 20-day breakout.

As with entries, the Turtles typically did not place exit stop orders but instead watched the price during the day and started to phone in exit orders as soon as the price traded through the exit breakout price.

These Are Difficult Exits

For most traders, the Turtle System exits were probably the single most difficult part of the Turtle System rules. Waiting for a 10- or 20-day new low often can mean watching 20 percent, 40 percent, or even 100 percent of significant profits evaporate.

There is a very strong tendency to want to exit earlier. It requires great discipline to watch your profits evaporate so that you can hold on to your positions for the really big move. The ability to maintain discipline and stick to the rules during large winning trades is the hallmark of an experienced successful trader.

Tactics

The architect Mies van der Rohe, when speaking about restraint in design, once said: "God is in the details." This is also true of trading systems. There are some important details that can make a significant difference in the profitability of your trading when you are using the Turtle trading rules.

Entering Orders

As was mentioned before, Richard Dennis and William Eckhardt advised the Turtles not to use stops when placing orders. We were advised to watch the market and enter orders when the price hit our stop price. We also were told that in general it was better to place limit orders than market orders. This is the case because limit orders offer a chance for better fills and less slippage than do market orders.

Any market at all times has a bid and an ask. The bid is the price at which buyers are willing to buy, and the ask is the price at which sellers are willing to sell. If at any time the bid price becomes higher than the ask price, trading takes place. A market order will always fill at the bid or ask when there is sufficient volume, and sometimes it will fill at a worse price for larger orders.

Typically, there is a certain amount of relatively random price movement that occurs, which is sometimes known as the bounce. The idea behind using limit orders is to place your order at the lower end of the bounce instead of simply placing a market order. A limit order will not move the market if it is a small order, and it almost always will move it less if it is a larger order.

It takes some skill to be able to determine the best price for a limit order. However, with practice, you should be able to get better fills using limit orders placed near the market than you do with market orders.

Fast Markets

At times the market moves very quickly through the order prices, and if you place a limit order, it simply will not get filled. During fast market conditions, a market can move thousands of dollars per contract in just a few minutes.

During those times, the Turtles were advised not to panic and to wait for the market to trade and stabilize before placing their orders. Most beginning traders find this hard to do. They panic and place market orders. Invariably, they do this at the worst possible time and frequently end up trading on the high or low of the day at the worst possible price.

In a fast market, liquidity temporarily dries up. In the case of a rising fast market, sellers stop selling and hold out for a higher price, and they will not recommence selling until the price stops moving up. In this scenario, the asks rise considerably and the spread between the bid and the ask widens.

Buyers now are forced to pay much higher prices as sellers continue raising their asks, and the price eventually moves so far and so fast that new sellers come into the market, causing the price to stabilize and often to reverse quickly and collapse partway back.

Market orders placed into a fast market usually end up getting filled at the highest price of the run-up, right at the point where the market begins to stabilize as new sellers come in.

The Turtles waited until there was some indication of at least a temporary price reversal before placing our orders, and this often resulted in much better fills than would have been achieved with a market order. If the market stabilized at a point that was past our stop price, we would get out of the market, but we would do so without panicking.

Simultaneous Entry Signals

Many days there was little market movement and little for us to do besides monitor existing positions. We might go for days without placing a single order. Other days would be moderately busy, with signals occurring intermittently over the stretch of a few hours. In that case, we would take the trades as they came until they reached the position limits for those markets.

Then there were days when it seemed like everything was happening at once, and we would go from no positions to loaded in a day or two. Often this frantic pace was intensified by multiple signals in correlated markets.

This was especially true when the markets gapped open through the entry signals. You might have a gap opening entry signal in crude oil, heating oil, and unleaded gas on the same day. With futures contracts, it was also extremely common for many different months of the same market to signal at the same time. In those moments it was important to act efficiently and quickly while trying to keep from panicking and issuing market orders since that invariably would have resulted in much worse trade fills.

Buy Strength, Sell Weakness

If the signals came all at once, we always bought the strongest markets and sold short the weakest markets in a group.

We also would enter only one unit in a single contract month at the same time. For instance, instead of buying February, March, and April heating oil at the same time, we would pick only the contract month that was the strongest and that had sufficient volume and liquidity.

This is very important. Within a correlated group, the best long positions are the strongest markets (which almost always outperform the weaker markets in the same group). Conversely, the biggest winning trades to the short side come from the weakest markets within a correlated group.

The Turtles used various measures to determine strength and weakness. The simplest and most common way to do that was simply to look at the charts and figure out which one "looked" stronger (or weaker) by visual examination.

Some Turtles would determine how many N the price had advanced since the breakout and buy the market that had moved the most in terms of N. Others would subtract the price three months earlier from the current price and then divide by the current N to normalize across markets. The strongest markets had the highest values; the weakest markets had the lowest.

Any of these approaches will work well. The important thing is to have long positions in the strongest markets and short positions in the weakest markets.

Rolling Over Expiring Contracts

When futures contracts expire, there are two major factors that need to be considered before rolling over into a new contract.

First, there are many instances when the near months trend well but the more distant contracts fail to display the same level of price movement. Do not roll into a new contract unless its price action would have resulted in an existing position.

Second, contracts should be rolled before the volume and open interest in the expiring contract decline too much. How much is too much depends on the unit size. As a general rule, the Turtles rolled existing positions into the new contract month a few weeks before expiration unless the (currently held) near month was performing significantly better than contract months that were farther out.

Finally

That concludes the Complete Turtle Trading System rules. As you probably are thinking, they are not very complicated.

However, knowing these rules is not enough to make you rich. You have to be able to follow them.

Remember what Richard Dennis said: "I always say that you could publish my trading rules in the newspaper and no one would follow them. The key is consistency and discipline. Almost anybody can make up a list of rules that are 80% as good as what we taught our people. What they couldn't do is give them the confidence to stick to those rules even when things are going bad."

Perhaps the best evidence that this is true is the performance of the Turtles: Many of them did not make money. This was the case not because the rules did not work; it happened because they could not and did not follow the rules.

The Turtle rules are very difficult to follow because they depend on capturing relatively infrequent large trends. As a result, many months can pass between winning periods, at times even a year or two. During those periods it is easy to come up with reasons to doubt the system and to stop following the rules: What if the rules don't work anymore? What if the markets have changed? What if there is something important missing from the rules? How can I be really sure that this works?

One member of the first Turtle class, who was fired from the program before the end of the first year, suspected early on that information had been withheld intentionally from the group and eventually became convinced that there were hidden secrets that Rich would not reveal. That trader could not face up to the simple fact that his poor performance was due to his own doubts and insecurities, which resulted in his inability to follow the rules.

Another problem is the tendency to want to change the rules. Many of the Turtles, in an effort to reduce the risk of trading the system, changed the rules in subtle ways that sometimes had the opposite of the desired effect. Here is an example.

Sometimes a trader fails to enter positions as quickly as the rules specify (1 unit every ½N). Although this may seem like a more conservative approach, the reality could be that for the type of entry system the Turtles used, adding to positions slowly might increase the chance that a retracement would hit the exit stops, resulting in losses, whereas a faster approach might allow the position to weather the retracement without the stops being hit. This subtle change could have a major impact on the profitability of the system during certain market conditions.

It is important to build the level of confidence you will need to follow a trading system's rules. Whether it is the Turtle System, something similar, or a completely different system, it is imperative that you personally conduct research by using historical trading data. It is not enough to hear from others that a system works; it is not enough to read the summary results from research conducted by others. You must do it yourself.

Get your hands dirty and get directly involved in the research. Dig into the trades, look at the daily equity logs, and get very familiar with the way the system trades and the extent and frequency of the losses.

It is much easier to weather an eight-month losing period if you know that there have been many periods of equivalent length in the last 20 years. It will be much easier to add to positions quickly if you know that adding quickly is a key part of the profitability of the system.

BIBLIOGRAPHY

Online Sources

The following sources are available to anyone who wants to learn more about trading and trading system development:

www.wayoftheturtle.com: my personal online blog and discussion site.

www.tradingblox.com/forum: a trading forum that I moderate and manage at my software company.

www.modustrading.com/turtle: a trading education site run by my friend David Bromley, who offers courses for those who want to learn about trading and system development. I helped him develop part of the initial curriculum and keep hearing good things about it from those who have taken his course.

Suggested Reading

In the course of writing this book, I wanted to make sure that I had a good sense of what had been written about trading and trading system development, and so I tried to read or reread most of the books written on trading over the last 10 or 15 years that were on the recommendation lists of people I respected. I found the following books especially useful:

Conway, Mark R., and Aaron N. Behle. *Professional Stock Trading*. Waltham, MA: Acme Trader, 2003.

Elder, Alexander. *Trading for a Living: Psychology, Trading Tactics, Money Management*. New York: Wiley, 1993.

LeBeau, Charles, and David W. Lucas. *Technical Traders Guide to Computer Analysis of the Futures Market*. New York: McGraw-Hill, 1992.

Tharp, Van K. *Trade Your Way to Financial Freedom*. New York: McGraw-Hill, 2006.

Weissman, Richard L. *Mechanical Trading Systems: Pairing Trader Psychology with Technical Analysis*. Hoboken, NJ: Wiley, 2004.

Trading War Stories

If you like reading about real traders, you will find the following books interesting:

Lefèvre, Edwin. *Reminiscences of a Stock Operator*. New York: Wiley, 1994.

Schwager, Jack D. *Market Wizards: Interviews with Top Traders*. New York: HarperCollins, 1993.

Schwager, Jack D. *The New Market Wizards: Interviews with Top Traders*. New York: HarperCollins, 1993.

Additional Readings

Baron, J., and J. C. Hershey. "Outcome Bias in Decision Evaluation." *Journal of Personality and Social Psychology*, 1988.

Bernstein, Peter L. *Against the Gods: The Remarkable Story of Risk*. New York: Wiley, 1996.

Black, Keith. *Managing a Hedge Fund: A Complete Guide to Trading, Business Strategies, Operations, and Regulations*. New York: McGraw-Hill, 2004.

Crabel, Toby. *Day Trading with Short Term Price Patterns and Opening Range Breakout*. Greenwood, SC: Traders Press, 1990.

Feynman, Richard. *Surely You're Joking Mr. Feynman!* New York, W. W. Norton & Company, 1997.

Gilovich, Thomas. *How We Know What Isn't So*. New York: Free Press, 1993.

Kaufman, Perry J. *New Trading Systems and Methods*. New York: Wiley, 2005.

Keirsey, David, and Marilyn Bates. *Please Understand Me: Character and Temperament Types*. Delmar, CA: Prometheus Nemesis Book Company, 1984.

Kiev, Ari. *Trading to Win: The Psychology of Mastering the Market*. New York: Wiley, 1998.

Pardo, Robert. *Design, Testing, and Optimization of Trading Systems*. New York: Wiley, 1992.

Pllana, Sabi. "*History of Monte Carlo Method.*" Available at http://www.geocities.com/CollegePark/Quad/2435/history.html.

Plous, Scott. *The Psychology of Judgment and Decision Making*. New York: McGraw-Hill, 1993.

Rabin, Matthew. "Inference by Believers in the Law of Small Numbers. " Economics Department, University of California, Berkeley, Working Paper E00-282. Available at http://www.repositories.cdlib.org/iber/econ/E00-282, 2000.

Roston, Eric. "Hedging Their Costs." *Time*, 2005.

Stridsman, Thomas. *Trading Systems That Work: Building and Evaluating Effective Trading Systems*. New York: McGraw-Hill, 2000.

Wilder, J. Welles. *New Concepts in Technical Trading Systems*. Greensboro, NC: Trend Research, 1978.

Wright, Robert. *The Moral Animal: The New Science of Evolutionary Psychology*. New York: Pantheon, 1994.

INDEX